TRANSIT TO HEAVEN

TRANSIT TO HEAVEN

MY TESTIMONY FROM ALLAH TO CHRIST

Salma Said Ali

New Wine Press

New Wine Press
RoperPenberthy Publishing Limited
19 Egerton Place
Weybridge
Surrey KT13 0PF
United Kingdom

ISBN 978 1 905991 06 8

Typeset in 10.5pt Palatino
by Avocet Typeset, Somerton, Somerset TA11 6RT
Printed in the United Kingdom

CONTENTS

PREFACE

The purpose of this book is to reveal my Testimony from a child born and raised as a Muslim to a born again Christian, a child of God. To understand my journey, an outline of my life experience is crucial, therefore the book initially gives insight of my biography which explores my journey from childhood to a turning point into a believer in Christ. It ends with a focus to remain strong in Christ and obey His will.

This book is formed of 21 chapters beginning with my family background, education and career and phases of my life such as marriages and life as a single mother. Other chapters discuss big decisions such as moving from my native country to the United Kingdom as a complete stranger, a place where none of my relatives lived. From here begins my Testimony, exploring my life as a devoted Muslim and how I eventually converted to Christianity. The Testimony gives a detailed account of a series of revelations and wonders I witnessed through visits, visions and live miracles and wonders that Jesus Christ performed to reveal Himself to me. Such an example is His unique way of using lights, the sun, the moon, and the stars as signals when communicating with me, but there was also that particular star which was amazing. You will also discover how the pages from the Qur-an (Islam's Holy Book) opened themselves in front of me to confirm verses that speak of such lights as signals of God.

As the book digs deeper into more revelations, I explain about hearing the audible voice of God from the sky as He spoke in my native language and as He mysteriously responded to my question about Jehovah, as the revelations become more explicit you will discover how I received my first Bible, the New King James Spirit Filled Bible and what is God's will through me.

You will know how I practically tested those revelations before I surrendered and declared Jesus as God. Then my baptism comes in and the phases of tribulations I went through after renouncing my former faith. But how did I keep it all secret? Confession to my family did not go free, I had to face the canon to testify my case. The meeting with core members of my family, all dedicated Muslims, was like meeting the Judges in one against many. But was I also to blame for my mother's death because I became a Christian? I faced rejection but remained strong in Christ.

ACKNOWLEDGEMENT

I would like thank all the people who have agreed for their names to be mentioned in this book:

Mr Rod Layne
Mrs Lucy Samuel

My sincere apologies to Peter, Rod's friend and Miriam my friend for being unable to trace them as I write this book but I thank them both their contributions towards my journey no matter how small. I thank Miriam for being there during my Baptism and her support during my wedding and throughout my pregnancy.

I would like to thank Rod Layne, Lucy and Miriam for their moral support each in their own ways; Mr Rod Layne for his life and his obedience to God, the man the Lord had used to take me back to Himself. I thank him for his patience in dealing with me from the beginning of my journey to my new life as a believer in Christ. I also thank Lucy for her moral support during my tribulations and for keeping an eye on me in prayers when I had to testify my new faith to my family abroad.

May God bless them all. Amen.

CHAPTER 1

BACKGROUND

I was born and brought up in a small Island in the coast of East Africa called Zanzibar in 1962. After the union with the mainland Tanzania, Zanzibar became a province of Tanzania although ruled by its own government. My family is said to have originated from the Middle East possibly from Oman and the Yemen. I grew up in a small family of a mother and three siblings, two girls and a boy. I lost my father when I was six years old during my first year in school, therefore I remember very little about my father. His long time illness in kidney failure led my mother to be sent home by her in-laws to live with her parents according to their customs, which could have been the reason for my not remembering my father clearly as it all happened when I was very young. However, the occasional visits my mother always paid to my father before he passed away helped me to at least remember his complexion and a long white gown he used to wear. As I became mature I tried to find out more about him from my grand-mother, my auntie and my half-sister, his first born, who told me that my father was well educated and smart. He was fluent in both English and Arabic and could read and write very well. She said he was light skinned and handsome, so her description about his complexion matched what I would see when I was a child when my father stretched his hands to give me my favourite snacks he would buy from the road. My auntie told me that their parents and grand-parents were wealthy merchants from Arabia, who crossed over through

Somalia in their journeys, where their father was born and continued their merchandising to Mombasa in Kenya where their father met and married their mother and finally ended their journey to this little Island in Zanzibar and decided to settle for the rest of their lives.

Although my mother was left to bring up the three children alone after the death of my father, she didn't receive much help from her in-laws, even contributions from our inheritance from our father that he had left from his own property, the hectares of land with clove plantations that he owned and which were sold for export. So my mother worked hard as a single mother to support us but thank God for her family around her, especially one of her four brothers, the landlord who supported her in many ways; and because of my mother's close relationship with her family we grew up very close to all our cousins and even though we were poor, we were happy and grew up with brotherly love for all our cousins from my mother's side.

I started school when I was 6 years old and finished Secondary School with high grades, which enabled me to get to one of the best High Schools in the country. I was one among the elite groups of high achievers in the School and my teachers and I had high expectations of completing my studies with high grades. However, my achievement at the High School did not come out as expected because of an early marriage at the age of 17, which was then followed by giving birth during the exam times, so I did not come up with the expected grades in my 'O' Levels, just with one 'C' and a few 'D's.

I must admit I wasn't forced into the marriage neither was it arranged for me as this is not practiced in my family, it was rather my own desire to marry someone I had known and loved at 16 who had a common interest with me in education. So despite my mother's concern about the marriage, especially because of rumours about his family, I followed my heart and got married to a person I knew even though I was still at School. He was 25 and I was 17 when we married, in reality I was too young to think better, I wish I had given myself time and a chance to grow, even though the heart was calling there needed to be a balance of measure before I committed myself into a serious relationship. I wish there was someone out there or some kind of service that could give a vision to young people before they commit themselves into serious relationships like marriage at an early age, especially when it is most likely that the young girls would be the ones left out to bring up the children alone. Having said this, I never regretted my marriage at that time but the consequences that were involved in it and how much I suffered as a young child.

The exams started just a few days after I had given birth to my first baby so I couldn't sit for my exams, which made me so upset seeing my peers taking their exams but I was left at home recovering from child birth. I did not accept this in my heart so as soon as I felt better, around about 10 days later I went back to School to sit for my exams. Unfortunately I couldn't do better, it was uncomfortable for me to sit down for long hours as much as I tried, so as a result I didn't achieve well, I only came out with a grade 'C' and a few 'Ds' for the remaining exams that I managed to catch up with. That disappointed me, especially when I thought of my peers in my group knowing that they would achieve well. I was truly sad and disappointed but appreciated my child and my marriage; however I also knew that it wasn't over with me, education was my only way, so I contended with myself and strived to take up private studies to re-sit the exams and although it took me two years to achieve the grades, it did happen.

At the age of 18, I joined the Teacher Training College in Zanzibar and achieved my Professional Teaching Certificate at the age of 20. As soon as I qualified I was employed as a Primary School Teacher in my local area where I taught for two years before I was promoted to teach in one of the best Secondary Schools in the country where I practiced for 5 years before I left for Britain.

During my time as a teacher I was also a wife and a mother who experienced very difficult times with the in-laws. In contrast to my own family, my husband came from a large family of a mother and a father and ten siblings. What

11

I did not understand before I was married to him was their family tradition of arranged marriages, which meant that their spouses had to be arranged for them by their parents. Therefore based on this tradition his parents had already set for him three of his cousins to choose from. It was believed that anyone out of these cousins would please his family, especially his mother and father who were themselves cousins. However, it seemed he had already decided to take a different approach and chose a different person who was not related to him, so he proposed to me instead. I came to understand more of this whilst in the marriage, especially when one of those cousins would approach me aggressively to establish her point, but thank God it didn't get to physical abuse, she had her own ways of making sure I wouldn't be comfortable with her. However, I was always sure that my husband only took her as a cousin and nothing more. Out of the remaining two I could assume that one didn't even care much about him because there were no stories about her but the other one once gave me a verbal assault as she walked past my house. These people lived not too far from us, in fact the more aggressive one was my neighbour while I was a teenager, living in the same block as me before I was married to her so called fiancé. So she knew all about my Maths tuitions from him when he used to come to our house to help me with my Maths. So because he broke the rules hate overflowed all around his family, including from those expected to marry him with their families; but their parents remained intact because after all they were more or less brothers and sisters or close cousins. For these reasons I was mistreated and taken as an outcast by the entire family and even his relatives, except one of his brothers who did not mind it all or perhaps managed to hide his feelings very well. The other person who would not be drawn into this was one of his other cousins, a lady who did not see any faults in me. His younger siblings were taught about this as they grew up. I was not welcomed by this family let alone loved. My mother was right after all.

The battle began not long after I got married when my

husband was given a scholarship to go for Higher Education in the capital, Dar-es-Salaam. On his second year of study, his parents invaded my home, the flat I shared with my husband and turned it to their own home without consulting me. They forced themselves in because the flat belonged to their son, so they were the ones to make decisions not their son, let alone consulting me. They saw my place as a wasted space whilst they had a large family to accommodate, so the whole family moved into my flat and you can imagine living with a family that disregards you. They used the arguement of needing the space because they were so many, I later came to understand that was not the true case, it was a planned mission to break my marriage.

As the flat was taken, my bedroom was then occupied by my mother-in-law and father-in-law and my kitchen was converted into a bedroom which I was made to share with two of my sister in-laws. This way I was made to live with them for a long time until my husband graduated from his study. My life was always worse when my husband was away from home; jealousy, anger and mistreatment were part of my everyday life with his family. My father-in-law was not even ashamed to announce publicly in the street that he would do whatever he could to end my marriage with his son, as he did not approve of it from the beginning. His announcements were heard and witnessed by many people in the street we once lived in, but my strength was that love I saw and experienced from my husband which I must confess was true, he loved me so much and because of this he had broken the family rule which created the tension and selfishness and an open plot to break up the marriage.

At the end of his studies he graduated and returned home; this was when we came to live together again in a different place in the town a few miles away from our previous home which his parents invaded. However, even though we were eventually living together, it didn't end the tension inflicted on us from his family and by any and all means they could. My first child was born when I was 17 and when he was 18 months old, he became sick for a few months and because of this my in-laws told me that my breast-feeding was causing his sickness; so they would take him away from me and bring him up with them instead. I had no say even if I didn't like it, but they used a manoeuvre that this would ease up my tension of running round to College and bringing up a child at the same time so it pleaded to me and I believed that they cared for me and my child. I must admit that they loved their grand-child, my son, despite everything else, so I didn't think it was a big issue at that time as this behaviour of grand-parents bringing up their grandchildren is very common in our country. However, as a 17 years old not knowing what was in their true minds, I let go of my child to be brought up by his father's family, I did not realise I was making a grave mistake. I also thought I wasn't far away from him and would visit him regularly. As I lived with my husband I discovered it was his normal duties to pay regular visits to his family every day and after all it was a routine for us to be at his family's home very often, so I could always see my child all the time. His young uncles would also bring him home to us as a normal routine. So my child was in good hands and loved by the whole family, he wasn't their problem.

After 3 years of fluctuations in the marriage, my husband went to Oman in Arabia in the hope of tracing his roots and finding a better life He told me he was going to sort our lives out and would come back for me when everything was sorted, so we should live together in peace far away from home; but this did not turn out as expected because even though he was in a far country his parents would not give up, in fact it got even worse for us. The thought of me going to live in Oman was seen as good fortune by his family, they would put their feet down to stop me from joining my husband; everything from telling lies to insulting me, as once my father in-law said to my best friend, ensuring that I will get the message, that I was not supposed to live in Oman because I did not have the right nose! In the end after 5 years of immense pressures my husband listened to his family's demand, he was forced to sign off the divorce papers and the marriage came to an end. One of his close relatives who happened to be there at the time told me he signed off the papers in tears, satisfying his parent's demand.

I was 22 years old with two young children when I was divorced. This was no doubt the most difficult time of my life breaking up with my husband. I was badly disappointed and was in pain for a long time remembering our life together and the promises he would give me about our future life together. In fact, the divorce papers arrived just before I set off for my exams so you can imagine the situation I was in. I thank God for my mother, she was the best comfort to me in these difficult times; she played a crucial role as a mother, counselling me and giving me hope, telling me that it wasn't the end of the world. She was always part of my grief, whatever phases I went through during my marriage, to the point she could not tolerate it any longer, but she would also see that love my husband had for me and so she kept her patience.

Soon after the divorce, my second child was also taken away from me when he was 2 years old. I was 20 years old when my second son was born and was living with my mother while my husband was away in Arabia. To take this one away, there was no consultation from the husband or the in-laws, but an order that I should bring my boy to his father's family to be brought up by them; since while he remained with me it meant that the money his father sent to his family had to be shared with me to support the child, and this would not be tolerated by my dominating father in-law. It seemed that my child's father agreed with his family to take my child away without my consent, and as the father has more right to the child than a mother, I had no say. Therefore all my children were eventually taken away from me and brought up by their father's family from their early age; the first one was only 18 months old when he was taken away and the other one was 2.

As a young mother, a person who had no power over her own children, I was instead left to visit my own children during school vacations, I had to 'borrow' my children to come home with me at certain times. Despite that the custom gives the father more power over the children the law also rules that the mother can still remain with the younger children

15

until they reach the age of 7 before the father can formally take them away; but I was given an order by the grandfather, he wouldn't consider anything else for me. I was bitterly upset about this whole thing especially when my husband, the person who loved me also agreed with his parents and would not even say anything to me. Whenever I visited my children they would be happy and eager to come home with me, but their faces would always sober when I returned them to their grandparents, especially my second boy who wasn't used to living with them from the beginning. This one would always think I went there to take him home with me, they were both too young to understand I never wanted them to be there in the first place, but I wasn't given any chances. As I left the place he would stand at the door and cry, calling 'Mama, I want to come home.' It was difficult for me to turn back and look at him, I couldn't cope, my heart suffered badly, I was worn out by this but persevered to be strong for them, I could also not forget the comfort I was getting from my friends and their parents, sometimes saying to me, 'Salma, these are your own children, by all means they will come back to you', or 'You have peed these children out yourself, they will come back to you, be patient' and so on.

Despite my disappointments by the divorce and everything else these people had done to me, love still flowed in my heart for my husband; so I waited for 3 years to hear from him from Arabia, in the hope that he would return to me and keep his promise. I did believe he still loved me, after all, his departure to Arabia was to better our lives and the plan for our rescue so we would live together away from all the tensions. I also witnessed many battles he suffered fighting for our marriage, especially with his father, but I suppose he was overpowered by the strong forces, so he ended up living in Arabia without me. We finally divorced in 1984, our children were only 5 and 2 years old. Many people approached me proposing for marriage after that, including one Omani citizen who could have taken me to Oman where he was, but their answers was always 'no' because I only had one person I loved, my childhood love. My refusals depressed my mother, she was disappointed by my harsh responses to other people but was wise enough to leave it to myself; and so I waited for 3 years for my husband's return, but to no avail.

CHAPTER 2

RE-MARRIAGE TO A BRITISH CITIZEN

In 1987, at 25, I re-married to a British man who came over to Zanzibar to visit his family on holiday, so I joined him to live in the United Kingdom through marriage. This was a big decision for me to make but after a long wait for my children's father to return to me I had to let go and move on in my life. On the day of my departure, my two children, now 5 and 8 came to the airport with me, the older one thinking I was going to take them away with me. He was clinging very close to me that day looking at me in the eye. Knowing that I was leaving them behind made me very emotional, it was the worst day of my life, weeping in front of everybody at the airport but I had to let go and move forward. It was a sacrifice to me but I knew that my mother was there for them and I would always be in touch, I knew that one day I would have them back with me so I boarded the plane and took off. I landed in London in the United Kingdom on the 1st of November, 1987 where I have lived until today.

The British man I married was a middle-age man born and brought up in Zanzibar who had lived in the United Kingdom from his youth in the late 1950s; this was well before I was born. To be honest this was the greatest risk I had taken in my entire life to marry a stranger and follow him to a country I had never been or had any relatives of my own. Yes, I listened to my heart but this time I gave room to my brain, it was also the opportunity to follow my dream of furthering my education in England, and it came freely, so the door was opened for me and

I entered it, my dream in this aspect had indeed come true. This time I decided to marry a middle-aged man from the lesson I had learnt from my first husband. I was right on one hand that I was his first priority before his own family, on the other hand I didn't know what lay ahead apart from I had just married a stranger and followed a husband home.

On the second day of my arrival in the UK, we took a train home from London to Liverpool where my husband lived, and there was my new home. I did not find many people from my country but met a few gentleman from Zanzibar who were my husband's friends and their common-law wives, the people they lived with as husbands and wives without getting married; they were more or less of the same age as my husband or even older. Because of the age gap there wasn't much we could share or a chance of becoming friends, they were all older than me, though one of the ladies was more approachable and friendly, she visited me quite often and played a mother's role to me which I much appreciated, she even baby sat my first little girl so I could go to College which made her own grown up children suspicious of her because of the way she treated me and also my complexion. She told me her children thought she was babysitting her own grand-daughter but she wouldn't tell them the truth. They thought that their mother might have had me with her partner. This lady was so good to me, I thanked God to have someone like her in a strange country.

Adjusting to my life in the new country was not easy; I kept calling home very often and checking on my children. My husband was working full time on shifts, so on the night shifts I would be left home alone which I never experienced before, but I had to get used to it as that was the reality in my new life. I experienced different personalities and approaches from people and learnt that people are different in many ways. In the same year of my arrival, my husband took me to a nearby Community College to enrol for a course since he knew my ambition. In that place I met many foreign people from different countries coming to learn English. When I was interviewed, the Senior Teacher told me that I should join the Community College at their main Site near the City Centre to study GCSE's or 'A' Levels as my English was of a high level; but I decided to remain in the nearest Centre just to get used to the system first and adjust my English for the first year. My concern was though I could understand the teachers or my Doctor at the Surgery when they spoke to me, I found it very difficult to understand the local people in the streets which bothered me very much, so the teachers agreed with my decision and entered me for the Cambridge First Certificate for that year, though they explained to me that understanding people in the streets was nothing to do with my comprehension but the local dialect. In this Centre, I also learnt typing skills and achieved a Pitman Advanced Qualification and became a touch typist at 50 words per minute.

As I adjusted to my new home I found the local people in Liverpool friendly and approachable; people would be happy to say hello to their neighbours with smiley faces even though everyone would mind their own business and although I did not have any friends I adapted to the life style very quickly and felt comfortable. I followed my ambition and continued with my education in the mainstream College the following year and even though I had already achieved my 'O' Levels from home which were equivalent to the English qualifications, I re-studied the GCSEs in my favourite subjects in English, Maths and Geography and continued with the 'A' Levels after that. In fact, I didn't have any time to lose. The A/S Level in General Studies enabled me to obtain entry into the University as a mature student in the following years. In addition to these subjects, I also took some short courses in IT to update my computer skills.

In 1989 nearly two years after my marriage, I gave birth to my first little girl. I cannot forget the support I had received from my friend, the lady who took me like her own child and all the teachings for caring for my baby I had received from the mid-wives when I didn't have a clue of how to even bathe my own child, which made them ask me if I really had two children before her or I was joking. At home all these things were done by mother let alone being a teenager myself. Having this child made me feel peaceful and free, I was now a mother who could bring up her own child without anyone taking her away from me, though she wasn't a replacement for my other two children abroad. So I stayed with my child at home for six months before I returned to College to continue with my studies. My friend looked after my child like a grandmother when I went back to College.

Nearly two years after the birth of my little girl, I visited home for the first time and stayed there for 8 weeks during the summer holidays. Unfortunately, my two boys were no longer in Zanzibar when I got there, their father had come home and taken them to Oman where he lived. He told my mother to let me know he was taking the children with him to Arabia; and although I didn't see them when I went home my heart was at ease because at last my children were eventually living with at least one of their own parents.

In 1992, I gave birth to another little girl, angelic in spirit and always contented, a friend and a company to her sister. I continued with my life as a wife and a mother and continued to study and a year later I visited home for the second time, my mother was pleased with me and thought that I was all sorted and contented. I also knew that she missed me so much while I was away but there was not much she could do, she had to accept that I was married and lived far away.

No one knew about the character of my new husband, I kept it to myself and always prayed for the best. My peace of mind was also limited, I missed my children so much and although my husband knew about this he did not appreciate them coming over to live with me, therefore I felt trapped in a different situation and even though I had all I needed in my new home I could not be complete without my two boys also. Five years after I last saw them in Zanzibar, they came to visit me in the United Kingdom for the first time. This time they were 10 and 13. It was obvious that they had missed me, they told me that they wanted to live with me but it wasn't the right time for me to keep them at that time because they had only come to visit me on holiday and I hadn't consulted their father nor discussed with my husband properly; but I promised them I would take them back later.

My mother happened to come to England for treatment in the same year and so she managed to meet with my sons just before they went back to Arabia. This was the best time of my life, we were all together again and the children were very happy. However, during her visit in Liverpool, my mother had to stay in hospital for twenty days because of illness, when she was eventually cleared and allowed home this was the time when she really saw the true colours of my husband, everything about his behaviour came to the open so my mother found out the reality of my life with my new husband in England. Seeing my mother in the house, he went worse in his unreasonable behaviour. My mother could not take it again; she was certainly not happy and wouldn't accept it.

My husband was aggressive and full of jealousy, he wasn't supportive when the children were sick. My older daughter was diagnosed with asthma from a very young age and because of this I was in and out of hospital very often. To be precise I would be in hospital for one full week every two months because of her chronic asthma; but during these hard times her father wouldn't even come to hospital with me or even visit her when she was there. I would have to go in the ambulance on my own with her and stay in hospital alone until we were allowed home when her breathing became normal. So when I saw other children visited by their parents and relatives I felt so bad and was sad, I sometimes thought the nurses might even think my child had no father. I suffered a hard time when one time I thought I would lose my child alone in hospital when she went in a coma.

This man did not have a drinking problem, he would only have a drink for pleasure but jealousy provoked aggressiveness and his unreasonable behaviour. I suffered this for many years but always expected him to change. It was irritating at times when I wanted to take my children for a day out or even to the local park and he would say I was going to meet with my boyfriend. This behaviour started when I once gave him a message from his own friend who I happened to bump into in the City Centre, when I came home and passed the message on it provoked an argument that I meant to meet with his friend at the City Centre. I was insulted by this because I am not of that type, let alone meeting with a man who is old enough to be my father. As I grew up I valued my Islamic faith and would always have a relationship in the marriage otherwise I would stay away from intimate relationship with men. The problem with jealousy persisted and he would act the same way with any man I happened to bump into if I told him they said hello to him. It was very frustrating. Other clashes we had were about our faith as I came to know he was only a Muslim by birth and as a devoted Muslim I was offended when he wouldn't fast in Ramadhan; and even though practising his faith was only between himself and his God it had really affected my feelings about him. I then remembered what his mother once told me that I shouldn't cook for him if he didn't fast but he wouldn't understand that. I only came to know about his behaviour when I came to live with him.

My mother only came to visit us for one month but when he saw her in the house, his behaviour changed for the worse, he would not tolerate anyone else in the house. Sometimes he would even come home drunk something that would never done before and as he was doing this even in Ramadhan my mother had it all in the box, she witnessed everything herself, so I had my questions to answer, she had expected a good man. When I wasn't cooking for him because he wasn't fasting it would make him more aggressive, so things went worse in front of my own mother. However, she knew where she stood in the house, she was only a visitor and she wouldn't say a word to him. As he did these things I also remembered his good side and tried to be tolerant with him. I thought may be the presence of my mother might have made him insecure, perhaps he thought she was going to stay there forever!

While still married with him, I took up the Initial Teacher Training course for teaching Basic Skills in ESOL at a City College in 1993. Once qualified I started to work in Liverpool Community College as a part time ESOL Teacher on a one to one basis and also as a Learning Support Tutor helping out ESOL learners who came from different nationalities, especially from the European Community. Seeing how people struggled in learning a foreign language inspired me to specialise in teaching English for Speakers of Other Languages (ESOL), leaving my own teaching specialism I qualified from home as a Biology Teacher. I continued to work as a part time Teacher and took up opportunities to further my education to high levels as much as I could.

My relationship with my husband started to deteriorate as his unreasonable behaviour continued, despite my effort and prayers hoping for him to change, this went on for a long time and so our marriage formally ended in 1995. My point of no return began well before my mother came over to visit me when my child was in a coma for her bad asthma, and as much as I could tolerate him for not putting any effort at least for his own child, it came to an end when he aggressively said it was better if the child died so he could get some rest. When he spoke these words I finally knew I was living with a cruel man and was not going to be his wife any longer. From that day my heart turned away from him, I didn't want anything to do with him anymore and certainly not intimacy. I knew that I wasn't going to be with him much longer. My last straw was when he came home from work one day after his evening shift around 11:00 o'clock in the night when I was fast asleep. As soon as he got in he went to the kitchen and picked up the sauce pan with his dinner in it and came upstairs and threw all the food at me on the bed. There were no microwaves in those days so the food had to be in the sauce pan for him to warm up when he came home in the night, something which he would always do himself. When that happened I got up shocked and my mother stood up next to my bedroom door and seeing the food thrown on my bed, she called his name and said 'Are you doing this to my child?' He didn't say anything but went downstairs. My mother immediately said to me 'Salma, I want to leave this place tomorrow, so take me to London tomorrow; I don't want to stay here anymore.' Nobody slept well that night, it was very uncomfortable but nobody was hurt. The next morning I washed my children and took the older one to school as normal. My mother didn't know what was in my mind, she was just watching me. The time came and he sorted himself out and went back to work in the afternoon, this was when my mother said to me, 'Salma I don't want to leave this country seeing you living with this man, my heart is troubled.' I looked at her and said I am going to find help; you wait for me with the child!

There was no time to lose so I walked to the Law Centre nearby, this was the place near my home which I had been observing for a while. So I walked into the office and as it was all on my face the person took me to the private room where I reported it all. The lady at the office asked me if I could stay in my house for another day but I said no, I want to leave now. So she said go back in there and gather as much as you can take and they would come and collect me with my children before my husband returns from work. I trusted that and went home. I told my mother we would be leaving for a refuge place in a few hours. She said fine, as long as I see you safe. This was the day I knew about the Social Workers so after seven years of marriage the Social Workers in Liverpool helped me leave the house with my little ones into a secret place of safety, called the refuge house. This was where I was supported to find a property in London so that I could be far away from him, and so I ended up living in London, which has been my home since 1994.

Here we are once again, a single mother with two young children living in a strange city, though this time I was much more familiar with the system compared to my first journey from home. My experience of living in Liverpool for seven years helped me learn and adapt to the system in the country therefore I was ok settling in with my children in London. A year later, my boys also came to live with me in London so there I was a lone parent with four young children to look after but my mind was settled and my heart was contented. I was at last happy and safe with all my children.

CHAPTER 3

EDUCATION AND CAREER
IN THE UNITED KINGDOM

When I was finally moved to London the Council offered me a new home in the South East where I have lived since. I had to remain on welfare support for one year while searching for new employment but was eventually appointed as a part time ESOL Teacher in the local Community College near home. As I worked part time opportunities knocked for anyone who wished to develop their teaching skills so I joined the courses to enhance my skills. Despite being already a qualified Teacher with five years experience from home, my qualification was not accepted as equivalent to the Teaching Qualification in England so I had to take the qualification again to remain in teaching. I was motivated to become an effective teacher so doing the course again did not disturb me at all; as an ambitious person I took it for my own development so I was OK to learn new skills. Also being a lone parent did not put me off studying; in fact, it fuelled my ambition to achieve the higher education degrees I had wished for all the time. In the following year I achieved a Teaching Certificate in Further Education and then moved on to Post Compulsory Education and Training (PCET) in 1997.

Packed with work and parenting responsibilities, I continued to study part time and eventually achieved two University qualifications, which took me six years to complete altogether. I had used many years of my life in continuing education and finally had achieved a proper Teaching qualification, a Cert. Ed. for teaching in Post Compulsory Education and Training (PCET) followed by a Bachelor's Degree in Education and Training (BA ET) both from the

University of Greenwich; and as I obtained my qualifications, my reward was not far away, opportunities knocked, and in 1999 I was appointed as a full time Lecturer in Broadwater Farm Enterprise Centre, an Off-Site campus of a local Further Education College in Tottenham Haringey known as CONEL (College of North East London), where I worked full time for five years until I left for maternity leave in 2004.

A year later I returned to work part time in the main site teaching ESOL and IT and from there on I moved on to Teaching Programmes, starting with Access to Teaching within the same college, then to Diploma in Teaching in the Lifelong Learning Sector (DTLLS) elsewhere, where learners achieve Qualified Status in Teaching and Learning known as QTLS. As a result of my long time experience in the teaching profession, I have become an Internal Moderator and Verifier in my specialist subjects and also work as an External Examiner, now known as Standards Verifier, for BTEC Higher Nationals and as a Centre Quality Reviewer (CQR) for London and South East Regions approved by Edexcel.

CHAPTER 4

REVELATIONS FROM GOD
'THE SEVEN WONDERS'

However, during my time as a Lecturer in Broadwater Farm Enterprise Centre, the Off-Site of CONEL, I experienced teaching people from different communities and backgrounds, including people from the Caribbean; and in 2002 while carrying out my duties in the classroom, I came across a student who wanted to know why I had to wear a 'Hijab', a scarf covering my head down to my shoulders. I had to explain that it was necessary for me to cover my head because it is a requirement for Muslim women to cover their heads based on our Islamic belief. Later on I came to understand that this student was a Christian and in my group there were some more of his belief who would sometimes have discussions about Jesus Christ during their break times. Unexpectedly, my answer about my Islamic belief gave way to frequent discussions with him which sometimes drew others from the group to join in, those who had interest in talking about different faiths.

As time went by during the year the student, Rod, and I got ourselves more involved in discussions about Jesus Christ, basing the issue on our different faiths, Islam and Christianity. As a Muslim, I believed in Jesus known as 'Issa', as one of the prophets of God who served God the Creator faithfully according to Islam as it is written in the 'Qur-an' the holy Book of Islam; apart from this He does not possess any supernatural authority as the almighty God, or being the Son of God as Christians believe, because according to Islam God has no Son. As a Muslim however, I did believe in His supernatural birth, that He did not have a human father and that Mary, His mother conceived Him through the Word of God that came from the Angel Gabriel known as Jibril in Islam; but this in Islam is regarded as any other miracle from God such as how He created Adam, the first man on earth etc. As a Muslim, I believed that Jesus Christ did not die but was taken up alive by God, as God would not let His own Prophet be tortured in the way it is said. So these discussions uncovered different views of our beliefs and created the environment for further discussions but we were all happy to go ahead with them. As a devoted Muslim however, I would not let my 'religion' proved wrong, I took heed in giving as much information as I could and would be as rebellious as possible to protect my religion and also to win his heart. By this, I even tried to bring him a copy of the translated version of 'Qur-an' in English so he could see the decency of my information based on the Holy Book which is believed as the word of God in Islam. My friend however, refused to take the book or even touch it, when I told him here is the book, he waved his hands away and as if shocked he said, 'Oh no, I've got my Bible, it is enough' and went away.

While he found it difficult to convince me, I, on the contrary, I was inspired by his patience and the calm character. I was somehow willing to listen to his views but at the same time would not jeopardise my responsibility as a teacher to him. These conversations were only taking place during break times and could also involve other interested parties in the group; such as the one young lady I had nearly convinced to convert to Islam but was rescued by Rod. As a friend she was talking to me about her life experiences and how she thought she was rejected by her God but when hearing this Rod suddenly told her 'God has not abandoned you' and as soon as she heard this her attention was drawn to him and started listening to him instead. From this point onward, Rod started revealing her life story which somehow eased up her frustrations. Rod took it politely with me and started off by revealing my history, talking to me about my past experiences as a child and as a young person before I even came to the United Kingdom; this included even the lifesaving experience

I once practiced to save a little chick as a young person at home. He also told me about my dreams I had in the past, one of which was about the place that I saw I would be living at in the United Kingdom before I even came to the country. All the things he said about me were true and what amazed me was that he was neither around to witness my childhood life nor as a young person, we neither knew each other nor were born in the same country we only met in Broadwater Farm as a student and Teacher. He is a person whose ancestors came from the Caribbean and I was born and brought up East Africa.

As we talked about dreams that day, I discussed about one I had in 1992 in Liverpool which was about me walking barefoot in a country side, a place full of trees separated by a footpath in between passing a little cottage painted in chalk, the only one in the whole place. As I walked through the footpath, I took a glance inside the little cottage then moved on walking in the middle of the forest. As I walked through the forest, I noticed all the trees bowing down to me as I passed through them. This scared me a lot! And suddenly still in the dream but half awake, I felt the existence of someone standing beside my bed and saying to me 'Pray', as I dug deeper inside my quilt because of fear, I felt the person moving around the bed and started shaking it very hard saying, 'Pray'. I trembled and sunk deeper into my quilt from head to toe. When I had the energy to reply, I said, 'ok, I will pray,' but he kept shaking my bed and said, 'Pray'; so I said to him, from now on I will pray every day, please leave me alone. At around 3 o'clock in the morning, the whole scenario was over, and I was relieved. This dream scared me to bits and I was still shaking as I woke up. The following day I told my friend, my neighbour, a Muslim lady of Algerian background who suggested we went to the Mosque the following day and she would talk to the Sheikh, the Muslims' Priest about my dream. So I was keen to hear what it actually meant. As she promised, the next day my neighbour told the Sheikh about my dream after the afternoon prayer, unfortunately, the Sheikh said she should tell me that these kinds of dreams could only come to Prophets or people of high ranks in the faith, people who are very close to God by their deeds, like the Sheikhs etc. and I should not mention it to anyone else. So I never told anyone about this dream for all those years until this time in my conversation with Rod.

There were times when Rod wanted to talk to me about Jesus Christ but I could see he was worried to approach me let alone start the conversation, being aware of my rebellious attitude on that issue. Sometimes I wondered why he was involved in it so much but his calm approach somehow made me attentive and so we would end up discussing about Jesus again and again. Amongst other things he told me about my life history was a question of whether I had seen Jesus before in my life, which reminded me of another dream I had in 1995, this time it happened in London. Shocked and out of speech, I mumbled, 'Yes, I saw Him.' Then I told him all about it as outlined below:

'One night, in 1995, I was struggling to get to sleep in my bedroom because I was feeling very ill. The symptoms of my illness were similar to the ones I suffered in 1985 which were believed to be connected with witchcraft that somebody did to me so that he could kill me. It took me a while to recover from this illness at that time so seeing similar symptoms once again I was afraid it was all coming back to me. So as usual I prayed before I went to bed and asked my God to help me with this illness, so I continued with the prayers until I eventually fell asleep. At around midnight however, I felt somehow awake but half asleep when this Man suddenly jumped inside my bedroom through the window. I lived in a Maisonette on the 2nd floor of the building so it would be impossible for anyone to jump in from outside without at least using a long ladder and breaking in through the double-glazing, I was surprised! So I starred at the Man as He walked in through the window and took a close look of Him as He walked towards me on my bed. It was like I was drawing Him in my head. He was looking at me as He walked towards me and when He was very close to my bed, I suddenly said, 'Jesus it is You!' He didn't say anything but came straight to me and touched my forehead checking my temperature, He then said, 'Salma, how else shall

I help you!' Strange enough, I wasn't surprised when He knew my name, everything seemed normal, I just looked at Him. He then walked with me towards the window and I suddenly found myself flying on His back but as we flew I did not see Him, I just felt leaning on His back. He carried me to the nearest Church in my local area that night. At that time this Church was still under construction and the window frames were not yet fixed. As we got into the Church I walked around discovering the place while He was up swinging on the chandeliers on the ceiling, it was the same man I saw in my room. When I was inside the Church I saw some people sitting on the floor chatting in one of the rooms then the dream ended.'

My own surprise about this dream is that I was a Muslim, I believed in Allah and the Prophet Muhammed, so my prayers will only be dedicated to Allah and the blessings to Prophet Muhammad. As a Muslim, I would rarely mention the name of Jesus let alone in my prayers, I wouldn't even think of Him except knowing that Jesus, known as Issa, is one of the Prophets of God; so it is unusual for a Muslim to use the name of Jesus in their ordinary life as He is not the main Prophet but when I saw this Man, my mouth automatically called Him Jesus and I wondered how I knew it was Him? I expected my prayers to be answered by Allah, or at least if my mouth called the name of Muhammad that night but I was surprised that I saw Jesus instead, it was Jesus who came and my mouth called His name automatically. So during these discussions about Jesus with Rod this dream raised my question, 'Why was it that it was Jesus who came to me when I prayed for help and not Muhammad?' But I kept it to myself and after this incidence that night I just carried on with my life as normal and practiced my Islamic faith without doubt. I had totally forgotten about the dream until this day when Rod asked me if I had seen Jesus before.

There was also one occasion that someone not known to me, came to see me at work; a stranger asking my name outside the classroom. When hearing this I walked towards the door where he was standing and said, 'I am Salma, how

can I help you?' He said his name was Peter and claimed that
he did not come to see me by his own accord but the Lord had
sent him. I did not understand him so he made it clear that the
Lord had sent him to give me a message. I said to him I will
see him at break time, so he waited for me in the pavement
outside the classroom. By telling me 'the Lord had sent him',
I asked him who this Lord is. He said, 'The Lord Jesus' so I
asked him what his Lord wanted about me, he said, 'He wants
you to know Him.' I was really furious to be approached
by a man I didn't know and talked to me about his Lord, I
thought he was provocative and offensive, even deranged;
first by degrading God because in my Islamic belief God does
not speak to people but used His Angels in the past to send
His messages to the Prophets and second, I found out that
he was Rod's friend which made things even worse and as I
was talking to him, I saw Rod standing aside against the wall
listening attentively, so I asked him how did this man knew
my name if he hadn't sent him to me. He admitted that Peter
was his friend but said he had neither sent him nor told him
anything about me. How could I believe that? I gave him 'my
eye' and waited for his time while dealing with his friend. He
remained listening on the pavement and did not add a word. I
asked his friend the same question whether Rod had sent him
to me but he said it was the Lord who had sent him to ask for
me. I then told both of them off severely and even told them
about their belief in three Gods; as in my understanding these
are the Father, the Son and the Holy Ghost, I even mocked
them saying they believed in Ghosts, while I believe in one
true God, Allah. As the man was giving up, he looked at me
with teary eyes; I paused and looked hard at him and at that
moment it felt like I had known him from a long time ago.
Suddenly and strangely enough, light tears watered my eyes
too but I walked back to my classroom and the man never
returned to me again.

As time went by, it was apparent that I wasn't going to
agree with Rod's beliefs that Jesus is that one God we all
talk about, I thought I had put a full stop of it especially after
what I thought was the last straw with his friend, so I did

not expect to hear from him again. However Rod thought differently, on one occasion quite a while after our last conversation he came in again at break time and said, 'Salma, the Lord says He wants you to know Him', then he went on to say 'He wants you for Himself.' On hearing this, I was furious and gave him my eye, he knows this eye, and while astonished I asked him, 'What do you mean? 'What kind of people are you, I said.' He didn't bring out any words, he just looked at me so I said, 'what do you mean He wants me for Himself?' 'Yes, He wants you for Himself,' he said. This was indeed too much for me for that day so I didn't allow for anything more, so he knew what he had to do. Anyway, he gave me time to digest what he had said and after certain time he returned and waited on the pavement beside the classroom and as I came out of the classroom at lunch time, he approached me once again and said, 'Salma, Jesus said, He will show you that He is God.' You can imagine getting a kind of message like this after intensive work in the classroom and especially during my break time, so I quickly replied, 'He did?' Rod said, 'Yes, He said He will show you that it is Him.' I wasn't intimated, I was surprised and full of rebellious thoughts, I wanted to prove Him wrong so I said, 'OK, let Him show me.' He said 'OK', and I walked away; there was no time for more talking so Rod left as soon as he had passed the message.

After a certain time Rod came back to see me and said the Lord said I have to fast for seven days and He will show me things. He insisted that I strictly dedicate the week to God during the fast while indoors, such as in prayers and even not to watch TV for this particular week. I did not rebel against fasting, after all, a Muslim fasts for at least one month every year according to Islamic faith, so for me this was a simple thing to do. The only thing that disturbed me a bit was that this fast would mean I did an additional seven days of fasting on top of my usual month of fasting in Ramadhan; but that was OK compared to not being able to watch TV as I would miss my favourite programmes – especially Eastenders! I also had to answer some questions to my two daughters who were now teenagers between the ages of 10 and 13, especially the question of not watching TV with them that week. So my explanations to them were I was trying to find out a few things from God that week therefore I had to dedicate myself to God in prayers, in reading the Qur-an and fasting again for seven days. The children were a bit suspicious about this but would not interfere. So even though Rod is a Christian and I was a Muslim I listened to him as a challenge to see if what he had said would come true. So I told him I would dedicated myself to my God (Allah) with my normal prayers and reading the Qur-an; he said OK and so I prepared myself for that particular fast on these other seven days as soon as I completed my normal fast in Ramadhan as these particular conversations of knowing Jesus were happening in that month of that year.

A few weeks before I started the agreed seven day fast, Rod started coming in with Scriptures that he said Jesus told him to give me. I have recorded them as below:

Wednesday, 13th November, 2002,
(in Islam, it was Ramadhan 8)

It was in the morning when I was at work; Rod came in the classroom and gave me the Scripture from the Gospel of Matthew 13:16-17. This Scripture was in the form of a cut-out. It read as follows:

'But blessed are your eyes, for they see, and your ears, for they hear,
For verily I say unto you, that many prophets and righteous men have
desired to see these things which you see, and have not seen them;
and to hear, those things which you hear; and have not heard them.'

Thursday, 14th November, 2002,
(Ramadhan 9)

35

Rod came in the classroom and gave me this Scripture: Matthew 4:5-20, which was also in the form of a cut out; and as usual, Rod claimed he received a message from God to give it to me. He insisted that he was told I pay attention to verses 14, 15 and 16. The Scriptures read:

'You are the light of the world,
A city that is set on a hill cannot be hid
Neither do men light a candle and put under a bushel,
but on a candle stick;
and it gives light unto all that are in the house
Let your light so shine before men, that they may
see your good work,
to glorify your Father which is in Heaven.'

It was when I started the seven day fast I had agreed to after I completed fasting in Ramadhan, that I started to see in my surrounding areas and in the sky the 'Revelations from God' which I could only perceive to be performed or done by God Himself. These were visual demonstrations of miracles and wonders using the sun, the moon and the stars, the audible voice of a Man I heard from the sky which matched the voice of a Man who walked through my bedroom window and checked my temperature in a dream, the bright light without rays which appeared to me in a very close range in a thick fog, the huge Star that hung near the ground as I turned into my road, the Qur-an pages opening by themselves and stopping at a chapter confirming that lights (the sun, the moon and the stars) are signals of God, the mysterious way of receiving my Bible and 'The Visit' that separated my soul from my body. I saw all these things within those seven days that Rod said I was told to fast and during which Jesus would show me things. These seven wonders completed the cycle even though the miracles of lights still continue; so to put things into perspective, I will start with the visual displays of the lights which happened as soon as I started the fast.

The mystery of the lights are connected with the sun, the moon and the stars and would come in a sequence with clear meaning. The lights would appear in different places on different occasions, for example when I would be outside, or while looking outside from indoors and usually when on my way to work and from work. At the end of the day, when I would be indoors the moon or a special star on its own would rest above my roof or just adjacent to my house up in the sky. Sometimes there would also be a bright star alongside the moon resting at the same places by themselves or would be surrounded by a group of scattered stars near them resting in the same manner.

I started to notice the sun and the moon following me alternatively but many times the two would be together. These lights would follow me wherever I go and would escort me home every day. The moon would sometimes be accompanied by a special star adjacent to it or would be on its own but when I get home it would rest above my roof far in the sky or position itself adjacent to my home every night, with or without that special star near it. I was also able and still am able to spot the moon when it would follow me in cloudy weather because it would make itself visible to me. When it came to the sun and the moon following me in pairs they would position themselves opposite each other, one on each side and put me in the middle, but if the sun followed me on its own then the moon would certainly take over during the night.

The special star, which could be the one that sometimes appears adjacent to the moon, would sometimes take over on its own and escort me home in the nights instead of the moon. I can distinguish it from the rest because it is the brightest one which stands out from the rest. If this star followed me on its own, it would purposely attract my attention and make itself visible to me so that I knew it had taken over from the moon. Also the cluster of many stars would sometimes follow and rest at home as the others would do but would sometimes just gather themselves in the sky wherever I would be and would certainly go alongside me if I left the place and stop where I would stop. These stars sometimes would be many, scattered in the sky or sometimes in a small group, however, there would always be a line of about 3 stars in the midst of them and the rest would scatter around that line. There was one time when I counted a cluster of around 11 to 12 stars at home with that line of 3 in their midst, the rest were scattered around it. In fact, I initially tried to ignore these scenes thinking they weren't a big issue, after all, I didn't want to sound insane but strangely enough they wouldn't give me rest, they continued their business day and night everywhere and eventually managed to draw my attention as I became suspicious and started to investigate their behaviour.

As I started to formally investigate them, one day I noticed the moon positioned itself opposite my window parallel to the place where I always sit in my living room. In the living room, I will always have my curtains closed in my corner but the rest will always be open every day. So while sitting in my corner, I noticed my curtains slowly opening as if it was by the wind then my eyes looked straight to that moon outside my window and suddenly the curtains closed; believe me it wasn't windy that day. The same thing happened again after several minutes while I was still sitting there, it was as if somebody was making me pay attention to that moon.

I have many times seen the moon in the early hours of morning and during the day times. On one occasion there was a very large moon following me from early morning on my way to work, this moon would make itself known that it was following me that day and every time it did this it was like someone was behind it carrying out these actions. It followed me at my driving speed on the other side of the road and whenever I paused or stop at the traffic lights it would also stop and wait. As I drove along the road it followed by passing through the buildings along the road. There was one time when I had to stop at the lights and where my car was standing there were certain blocks of flats with an alley way between them on the other side of the road, so as I stopped and waited for the lights, my car happened to stand parallel to these blocks then I saw that moon waiting between the two blocks at exactly the same spot opposite my car. So if I looked left from my position I would see the moon standing on the air between the two blocks.

The next time it happened when I was driving in my local area and to be honest I was getting so frustrated of being escorted all the time so when I saw the moon ahead of me I decided to drive off from the main road into the street corners trying to escape from it, convincing myself it would never find me in that corner; so I parked the car in a street away from the main road and decided to wait and see but it only took a few minutes after I had parked the car before the moon appeared in front of me. I looked at it and to be honest I just laughed because it was like a hide and seek game, I said to it 'You found me', and although it hadn't spoken back to me, it felt like someone was playing with me from that moon and said, 'Yes, I did.' It is really rare to see the moon in the daylight but I always see it in different sizes and in different weather conditions, sometimes it was very large in gold colour or in its normal colour and sometimes in its bright normal size. When it is accompanied by the bright star adjacent to it, it would always be a half moon and would always be followed by many other stars scattered near them but a little distant from the special star.

The sun takes its turn every day, except of course when it is cloudy or in thick winter. As it is with the moon it would follow me everywhere until sunset then would hand over to the moon or that special bright star. In the weekends or on the days that I didn't go to work it would rest adjacent to the place where I would be until sunset.

When I noticed that these behaviours were ongoing, I decided to involve my family, starting with my two daughters. I asked them to spy on these lights and test the scenarios when we were out together, whether we were walking or driving and in fact it didn't take them long to discover the truth, the only thing was they were very excited. So a day came when I took them on a long journey to Tottenham to buy some Egyptian bedding stuff, so that day the girls were my spies on the road watching for the instances as they happened; and as soon as we left home, as we approached Woolwich in our local area, my younger daughter noticed the sun dazzling in front of us while we were waiting at the traffic lights and said, 'Look at that sun!' Then we all looked ahead at the dazzling sun but I said to them I will ask God to move that sun from there to another place and back, and you keep watching! Then as I said that I asked God in my heart to move the sun from where it was to another place and back and within a blink of an eye it moved away and returned to the same spot where it was in front of our very eyes, it happened very fast indeed. So the children saw this and were very astonished! They said, 'Mum it moved very fast and went back to where it was!' I replied, 'Yes, it did'; it was amazing! Here I was not only testing what I had already told them about being followed by these objects but to also see if God will actually do something when I ask Him to do, especially because I had already tried Him once on my own to move the moon from one place to another as it followed me in my journeys and He did so, He moved it from where it was to another place and brought it back within a blink of an eye but this time He moved the sun from one place to another in front of my children and they saw it. When we got to Tottenham, just about to get into the shop, my younger daughter said again, 'Mum, I think the sun is following us.' I said to them this is what I have been trying to tell you. This is what is happening.

Still to do with God's lights, my other experience was when I was driving to work on the A2 towards Hackney on a dual carriage way at 50 miles per hour with speed cameras installed on the road. Just before my exit there was a speed camera therefore I had to slow down as I approached it. As I slowed down I saw a bright light standing on the air on my right hand side parallel to my car, it was on its own and standing just about 10 metres from the ground and about the same length away from me, it was very close. It was foggy that day and in the midst of the thick fog it looked like the sun without rays and because it had no rays it would look more like a bright moon on its normal size as one would see it from the sky. This bright light stood out so brilliantly in the midst of the thick fog, it was as if it had chosen the right spot to be noticed because it was next to the speed camera and my next exit. Although it was so bright it was calm, it did not burn me. I was shocked however and slightly scared but it was amazing to see a kind of light like this out of nowhere so close to me. When I told Rod about this at work he seemed so pleased, just keen to hear the stories.

On the very same day, this time on my way home from work, I saw a very large star, which I first thought was a helicopter, just hanging about above the road as I approached my right turn home from the main road. So I looked ahead before turning and instead it was a very large star indeed hanging above the road I would take home. I watched it face to face because it was standing opposite me as I turned into the road. It was just about the height of a lamp post above the ground and as big as the size of a small car, like a Mini Cooper. As I approached it I thought it was not true, I thought it might have been a helicopter standing there because I was dazzled by the lights but in fact it was a real star like those we see in the sky at night but big and actually hanging just as high as a lamp post in my street. Again this one also chose the right spot for me to notice it, there was no way I could miss it or pretend I didn't see it. The size of it was not like the way we see stars in the sky but it didn't lose its brightness, I am not sure if I haven't seen the real size of a star when it comes very close. It was very bright. I was driving home so I was fully conscious and concentrating, I was not dreaming. When I knew it was a real star, the first thing that came into my consciousness was the symbol of Jesus when He was born in Bethlehem, so I said to myself, 'Oh my God! The symbol of Jesus' I got home and told the news to my daughters and to Rod the next day.

The revelations continued as I continued fasting, one day I heard someone speaking to me from the sky, again as I was driving to work on the A2 but well before the Hackney exit. To start with, this was a gloomy day for me, I was sad and mourning to myself about the length of waiting for my husband's visa since we got married in 2001. I was grieving about a lot of money I had spent for it and time and effort in dealing with lawyers and even facing the Barrister to sort out his visa but so far nothing had come to light, so I was just there driving and mourning on the road until it got to the point that tears were dropping from me non-stop; especially when I thought of what my new in-laws had told me on the phone a week before that my husband would instead go to his cousins in Sweden if it takes any longer, which got me really confused about the whole thing and was left to think if I had made the right decision to marry him in the first place. Remembering my past experiences with marriages I got very upset and tears dropped like showers while driving. It was while I was in this state that I heard a Man speaking to me from the sky, saying, 'I love you Salma, and I'm sorry, you'll get better.' He spoke to me in my native language, Swahili and was very compassionate; and as much as it seemed very far from the sky, the voice seemed very close, I could hear it loud and clear just as if it was just above me.

This audible voice sounded very similar to the voice of the Man who came through my window in 1995 and checked my temperature beside my bed when I was very ill. My mouth naturally spoke His name that day, I called Him 'Is it You?' He spoke to me in my native language and that's how I recognise His voice; yes, it was the same voice. So I rushed to work and as usual Rod was there so I passed on the news. He seemed astonished, and said, 'You did', and as I was repeating it a few times asking him if he'd ever heard a live voice like this as this was something very strange to me, he said, 'Yes, I hear that all the time.' So I asked him again, you mean you hear His voice from the sky all the time? He said, 'Yes', then I calmed down.

The next thing that came about as I continued with the fast was the Qur-an pages turning over by themselves to the verses teaching about the lights of God, that is the sun, the moon and the stars and referring to them as the signs of God; and if that is so, they then relate to the scenes of the same lights that I was experiencing. The most extraordinary thing I noticed in this particular occasion is the Qur-an pages turning over by themselves as if by a gentle wind. It happened when I was in my bedroom in the early night as one of the rules of this fast was not to even watch TV, so I was basically preparing myself to read the Qur-an, the translated version in Arabic and English, as at this stage of my life I had already completed reading the actual Qur-an written in the Arabic language since childhood and repeated it many times as a habit. As I grew older, I recited the Book almost every year dedicating the prayers to my dead relatives which is regarded as a favourable gift from anyone's Muslim child. So as I got myself ready to read the Book that day, I first placed it on the bed as usual and got onto my favourite place and leaned on my pillow, as I did this I saw pages of the Qur-an opening up by themselves one by one just a little faster than someone would open them normally. I watched this until they stopped on a chapter called 'Suratul Noor' which is the chapter teaching about the lights of God. The illustration of light in this chapter is related to the sun, the moon and the stars which are described as the signs of God; and as the pages stopped opening, my eyes were focused onto this verse which is translated as follows:

"We have already sent down to you verses
making things clear,
an illustration from (the story) people who
passed away before you,
and an admonition for those who fear God."

So according to this chapter and this verse from the Qur-an things have been made clear to me that God uses the sun, the moon and the stars as His signals, which could also be compared with what is said in Genesis 1, which I only came to know after I started reading the Bible, that God said He had made these lights for signs and wonders. So I remembered the One who asked me to fast and He will show me things, He will show me that it's Him, could this therefore be the One who had made these lights and uses them as He wishes? And as I dedicated the fast and prayers to my God (Allah) could it be possible that this God used the verses from the Qur-an, the Book I know from my belief to evidence the symbols He used to show me that He is God, as He had said well before the fasting started? The verse also connects to the Scriptures from the Gospel of Matthew that Jesus had sent me previously through Rod, which says that He has blessed my eyes that they see, and my ears that they hear the things that many Prophets and righteous men have desired to see them and hear them but have not seen them and have not heard them (Matthew 13:16-17); and as soon as I received these Scriptures then all the wonders of lights had started. So I started to put things into perspective.

I thought about how all this had started, I thought of what had been said to me before the fast and what was happening during the fasting and began to ask myself, 'Is Jesus really God?', and while in this mind I decided to test Him in my usual prayers as a Muslim. So one morning during my early morning prayer I asked Jesus and said:

> 'If you are really God, then give me your Book,
> I want to know what happened in the past,
> I want to know about the Book of Moses
> (which is called 'Taurat' in Islam),
> I want to know about the Book of David
> (which is called 'Zaboor' in Islam)
> I want to know about the Book of Solomon,
> and all the Prophets.'

After the prayer, I made my way to work. That day I did not see or hear anything on the way so I just got on with my job. However, just before lunch time, I saw Rod coming in the classroom with a carrier bag in his hand. He stopped near my desk and said, 'Salma, I've got to give you this.' I asked him what it was that he wanted to give me but he was just standing looking at me and kept repeating the same words 'I've got to give you this', he kept holding the bag to himself. He did not even stretch his hand out to give me whatever it was. So people were wondering about what was happening but knowing Rod as one of their class mates they just got on with their work. I then asked him again what was it that he wanted to give me but again he was just looking at me which I found very strange, I wondered why he was acting that way so I stretched out my hand towards the bag and he eventually gave it to me but still stood there without a word. When I looked inside the bag there was a Book. I said to him, 'It's a Book', he said, 'It's the Bible'. I was so excited and said to him, 'I prayed this morning for God to bring me His Book. Thank you.' At this point Rod got very excited and eventually managed to speak to me; he said, 'I'm sorry it's so old and the covers have fallen apart, I wanted to buy you a new one but I was told to bring you this one.' I said this is fine.

I took it home and hid it somewhere only myself and the children would know. I learnt that that Bible was The Spirit Filled Bible, from the New King James Version, the Fifth Edition from the original Hebrew Bible. It was apparent that Rod loved this Bible, which used to be his mother's, very much; and according to him he begged the Lord to allow him to buy me a new one of the same version because he thought it was embarrassing that the front covers and some glossary pages were all ripped apart but the Lord stressed that he should give me that one, the one He had told him to bring me. So I received this Book, the Bible, my Bible in a miraculous way because Rod was not with me in my house when I prayed asking Jesus to give me His Book if He was really God, and He did on the same day, glory be to Him. For me to receive a Bible gave me another point of thought because I did not expect to receive this kind of Book, as a Muslim I expected something else, but this is what was sent to me by Jesus who said to me fast and I will show you things, I will show you it's Me. This Bible has become my favourite Book, the one I always want to use, I am so attached to it. It is like a point of reference to me every time I remember how it came to me and who sent it to me and to save it from deteriorating I have recently bought a new one of the same version and kept that one as a reference and my treasure. Sorry Rod, but I'm made up with it, thank you anyway.

After witnessing continuous miracles that Jesus had said He would do, I started to consider His position in real sense, is He really God? Considering the things I had seen there was every reason for me to start questioning myself, after all, before Jesus said 'fast' and I will show you things, I will show you it is Me, I had never seen them before or seeing the moon or sun behaving the way they did and in fact, they still do. However, I kept it between myself and my daughters even though I had no doubt it had to be God. I remained silent for some time.

CHAPTER 5

THE VISIT

Then Rod came and told me, 'Salma, the Lord says He will visit you.' So far I had learnt that when Rod mentions the 'Lord' he actually means 'Jesus'. However, I was surprised when he said that the Lord will visit me because in my understanding God does not visit people, so I took it lightly but eager to find out if God really visits people, so the time came that night when I knew that whoever visited me was supernatural and extremely powerful because of the fear beyond expression that I felt in His presence. The whole thing happened well after mid night when I became half-awake from a deep sleep. At first, it started as if someone landed at my bedroom door like wind, the door then opened by itself and I felt someone in the form of a man physically walking into my bedroom and pausing just after entering the door. At that moment I felt my whole body trembling with great fear, the fear that I cannot compare with anything else. As I was in this state, I remembered to recite a Chapter from the Qur-an called 'Suratul Al-Qur-Siyyu' which is the most highly ranked prayers in the Qur-an that can help someone in fear of any kind, it is about requesting help from God from His Throne and expecting an immediate answer on whatever you are asking for. So I recited this as I trembled. However, it appeared that as I was reciting the verses one after the other, the Person in my bedroom was also reciting prayers in reply to each verse I recited, it sounded as if in Arabic language as He walked slowly towards me. It was like we were exchanging prayers, I recite a verse and He replies it with a verse just before I moved onto the next one. Well, I was just in great fear, I didn't know what He was actually reciting but it was clearly said in Arabic in the order of each verse I was reciting; and as I continued through the Chapter, He slowly continued walking towards me and pausing between the steps to allow a little time. As He did this, the fear in me increased, my body trembled to the utmost level that got me to the stage when I could hear myself automatically reciting words in the language I didn't understand! This language ceased as He got very close to me and at that point I lost control, I lost consciousness. I died. Then I saw myself departing from my own body and lifted up just about 2 feet above my body facing upwards towards the ceiling. As my spirit was up there, I could see my body still lying on the bed on the same spot I was before I departed from it and then I could remember everything. Then in a matter of minutes I saw myself gently returning into my body in the same position as I went up, so I returned to my own body in the way it was laid on my bed. There was no more fear after I had returned to my body. This Person then walked closer and closer to me and sat beside my head on my bed. He was invisible, I did not see His face or colour but a figure of a Man who came in like wind. After He had actually sat beside my head, it was all peaceful, no more fear. Then I woke up.

This was no doubt a 'death experience' to me, an out of body experience as a result of great fear. Rod did tell me that the Lord said He will visit me but I didn't know how awesome the experience was going to be. It was a real surprise indeed. The visit did not even take long to happen, just soon after he gave me the message. I know that that night someone supernatural, so great and powerful visited me which I will never forget in my whole life. His presence was awesome; His power can give life or take it away. It was practically demonstrated through my own body when my life was taken away for a few minutes. To see my spirit departed from me and lifted up from my own body then a few minutes later returned back to me is indeed extra-ordinary, it is supernatural. Take it this way, the person that was taken out of my own body was me and at the same time the body that was lying down on my bed below me was also me. That night I practically witnessed the difference between the spirit and the body when the two were separated from each other. I did not have to wonder that, that Person that night must have been God when I connect the experience of life and death I encountered in His presence. I'm sure He didn't mean to finish me off that night, I wouldn't be writing this book; He only said He was going to visit me! I have learnt that when a Christian person mentions 'The Lord' it refers to 'Jesus Christ' and recalling from what Rod had said beforehand it was Jesus who was going to visit me, and from this experience I discovered that the Person who visited me that night could also take away my life and give it back as He practiced it in my own body. I believe that apart from God no one else has power to take someone's life and give it back, that Person did that to me that night. Hang on a minute, I have just remembered this, in John 10:18, Jesus says 'No one can take My life away, I have power to give it away and I have power to take it back.' Could this be Jesus? He was the One who said He would visit me.

At the end of the seven day fast, I could not deny that I witnessed many miracles and wonders I had never seen or heard in my life until the time I had agreed with the fast that Jesus said I should do and He would show me things. He even said well before this agreement that He will show me He is God. So I measured from what I had been told to what had actually happened during the fasting and even after that. The miracles of lights I have been shown in different situations represent the signs of God which are confirmed even in the Qur-an but can also be tracked from the Book of Genesis in the Bible when God created those lights and said they will be used for signs, Genesis 1:14. These signs of God still work the same way with me since the beginning of the revelations when I agreed with the fast and God uses them as a guide for me to trace His presence around me wherever I go, or wherever I am; and sometimes He will use them for my directions for example if I lost my way somewhere He will position the moon or a bright star to lead me the way. I have tested these signs with different people many times and most seemed to see the signs and agree with what I was saying but believing it would be from their own hearts. To close this, God also told Rod that I will continue seeing these things for the rest of my life, as I indeed do. So the work still continues.

One can always argue that the moon, the sun and the stars are ordinary lights and they are there for everyone, as my son once said to me, but I had also tested a situation with him on one occasion when I asked him to watch the moon from where we were until we got home and then to check where it would be waiting when we got home. As he realised that the moon was really following us until we got home, he parked the car outside our garage and said he was busy rushing somewhere else, so he did not come upstairs where he would be able to see the moon standing in the sky opposite our house through the living room window; and although he did not say anything along the way he could not deny the experience because he saw it all. The moon stayed opposite our house until dawn when the sun took over, waiting to accompany me back to work the next day.

CHAPTER 6

CONVERTING TO CHRISTIANITY

After all these ongoing revelations, especially those I noticed in the seven day fast, I accepted that Jesus is who He claims to be, the true God, because no human being not even Satan, the devil, can do what I have seen done, I believe no one can operate God's lights except Himself. These are the objects He said in the Book of Genesis that they be used for signs, so Angels would have to obtain permission from Him to use them, but He said to me well in advance that He will show me it is Him before all these wonders had happened, and the fact that I had to fast for seven days despite my usual fast of Ramadhan. Seeing the challenging prayers being answered, sometimes immediately, made me wonder, such as what I did with the children when I asked God to move the sun from one place to another on different occasions, just to prove to my children what I see, and He did that in a blink of an eye, and when He moved that moon from one position to another in front of my eyes.

The audible voice I heard from the sky, which is the same voice that I once heard from Him when He came through my window in my dream, long before these revelations began proves it to be Him. When He walked to me I naturally called His name saying, 'Jesus it is You', He came and checked my temperature, He spoke to me and said, 'Salma, how else shall I help you.' So I know Him because I've seen Him that night and He spoke to me so I know His voice as well. But if you wonder how I knew it was Jesus, well, my mouth just said His name, it was automatic.

The Qur-an pages, opened by a gentle wind in my bedroom, proved the lights as the signs of God and seeing what I had seen I asked Him in my prayer as a Muslim to bring me His Book if He was really God. I was alone in my own house when I prayed and the Bible was brought to me at work the same day; then I wondered why it wasn't the Qur-an instead, the Holy Book I know. Let alone that remarkable visit that night, how awesome and what a great power. His presence departed my spirit from my body, they couldn't hold on to each other, but the out of body experience didn't cause me any pain; hallelujah. This was the day I practically understood that the body is only a shelter covering someone who actually lives in it. This is something not easy to forget, I will remember it forever.

When the seven day fast was all over, I came to realise that Rod was actually fasting for me from before the beginning of the whole process. He then told me he actually started fasting well before he approached me about the whole thing. As a Muslim this raised a question to my understanding of the Christian fast, which I believed they are supposed to do 40 days each year, but that this was removed from the Bible because many did not feel comfortable with it. I also believed they would remove whatever they wished from the Bible and leave what they feel comfortable with according to their convenience, so if something is inconvenient for them to practice, such as fasting, they would simply remove it from the Bible. As a Muslim I also regarded a Christian fasting as something unworthy or with no meaning because I believed Christianity to be a false religion made up by men, therefore no wonder the Bible had been changed frequently. I wasn't aware that Christians could fast any time or for different purposes or a belief that their fasting could be led by God. So when I asked Rod why he was fasting, he said, 'I'm fasting for you.' I asked this during the seven day fast but in fact he had started fasting well in advance once he was given his assignment with me. So he was also asked to fast for me as the process was about to start. At first his reasons behind this did not register in my mind until the whole thing was over, then I came to understand that dealing with situations like these would need a strong back up, a spiritual back up; and me being asked to fast myself then witnessing all those miraculous interventions bridged the gap. I felt the strength of the Christian fast that it is not always empty, but more like a backup for a specific prayer.

In the end, despite the fasting being over not much had changed concerning the lights, in fact, they have never given up. So I told Rod what I thought about Jesus and accepted that He has to be God, because of what He had said to me from the beginning and what He had done to prove Himself to me, so He kept His word. Glory be to God. I now feel so ashamed of myself that I even let Him who is above everything go through all the hassle just for me to know it was really Him; but then if He didn't reveal Himself the way He did and performing stuff that could convince me, Rod would stand no chance in front of me and I would still be in darkness. I just thank God for redeeming me and also Rod for his life, for obeying God and allowing himself to be used for my salvation, amen. I have always believed there is only one God, prayed to Him and worshipped Him but I didn't know Him or have relationship with Him; but when the Bible says that Jesus is God who came in flesh in the Person of Jesus Christ, I believe it now because He revealed Himself to me in different ways just to convince me, and I saw how He looks like as a Man face to face when He checked my temperature and carried me to Church on His back. So if He is really God, what then would be really difficult for Him to do, if He is that Creator of Heaven and Earth would it be difficult for Him to make Himself into a Man?

As I moved on in my life I decided one day to visit my other son and his wife in Barking. So I took my daughters and drove to his place. As I was there I decided to explain to them about what was going on in my life hoping they would understand me. So I sat down with them and told them the whole story. When they heard about it my daughter-in-law suddenly asked me, 'Mum, are you alright?' Her first impression was I was losing it; but knowing that my evidence is only outside their window, I continued telling the story and showed them the moon which was standing outside their flat opposite the living room parallel to the spot where I was sitting in their living room. I also told them to examine it when I go to bed and notice where it would be. The girl agreed, so when the time was up we all went to bed; but as soon as I got on the bed I noticed the moon was already there positioned itself opposite my bed in the sky, I could see it through the bedroom window. So I called my daughter-in-law to come and look at it to prove what I was telling them. When she saw that it was true, that the moon suddenly moved from the other side to opposite the bedroom window she was shocked and got really scared. The first thing she said was, 'Mum, isn't this Gog – A – Ma – Gog?' She thought it was what is said in the stories of Islam that in the last days there would be situations happening that are to do with Gog and Magog. It was obvious that she didn't know much about Gog and Magog but she had some understanding about them from Islamic stories so she thought that moon was to do with it. So she called her husband straight away and told him about it, so my son came in and saw the moon shining brightly towards my bed. He was surprised with no doubt but he is a man. His wife however was still shocked and went on to say this might be the one that will resurrect dead people in the last days! But it was only that moon shining brightly from above towards the bedroom I was sleeping in that night. I just wanted them to notice that these lights do some mysterious things with me.

The next day we went out for a walk to a local park; so we chose a spot and sat down but as soon as we sat down we saw a very large moon hanging in the air very close to the ground. My daughter in law looked at it and said, 'My God! It's very big.' Remembering what happened last night she looked at her husband and we were all mesmerised by the size of the moon and how far down it was from the sky, the truth was obvious in their faces even though it was hard to accept, the moon appeared at the park in day light and very large in size and just stood close to the ground in front of us. I once again told them I see these things everyday hoping that they would link yesterday's situation to this one or at least appreciate these wonders from above but they actually thought I was deluded.

The next day I went home with my daughters; not knowing that they would gather together with my older son behind my back and take things to my brother, who've never had a good relationship with me since his marriage, this is someone who kept his distance from me, his sister and could not care less. However, despite his normal attitudes to me he actually cared and listened to my sons' request and visited me at home. This was a surprise to me as I hadn't seen him for quite a long time, he rarely visited me. Anyway, I welcomed him and he explained his purpose for the visit, which was to explore what he heard from my sons about my experiences, so he said he came in to check on me to make sure I was alright in mind. That day he also asked me if I was still in my Islamic faith or had already converted to another faith. I told him I was still a Muslim and was sure my mind works perfectly well. He said, yes you are, because a person who is out of their mind does not speak like that. They were all relieved and he went home.

On the 24th February 2003 Rod came to see me at work with a Scripture from the Book of John. He said to me, 'Salma, God said "Read John 3, the whole Chapter".' There was no need for me to test him or even question him anymore after all that I had gone through, so I just went home and read it and found that it was about the new birth. This Scripture was sent to me well after those miracles and wonders I had encountered during the seven day fast, which led me to believe what I saw and heard could not be done by an ordinary person or even Satan himself even though he was made by light; because there are certain things that one would know by their practice that they are not from God. On the other hand, God's own revelations are certain and can be distinguished from false episodes because false episodes would not continue in the way God does it. God has kept His word to me when He said I would see things throughout my life as they still do. So I knew in my heart that it had to be God especially when He preceded His words with Scriptures He had sent me beforehand. I believe He blessed and opened my eyes when He sent me Matthew 13:16-17, preparing me for those miracles and wonders and to be able to hear Him. So, the Chapter in John 3 that He sent to me was actually asking me to be baptised; as one of the Scriptures in that Chapter says, 'Unless one is born of water and the Spirit, he cannot enter the Kingdom of God', (John 3:5). So because of His love, God wanted to wash out my sins so that I could enter the Kingdom of God; and for this, He sent the Scripture from John 3 to inform me about being born again; which I had no idea about it.

Up and until I received this Scripture I had kept all the discoveries to myself, even though I believed it was the work of God. When I saw the words, 'Unless one is born of water and the Spirit, he cannot enter the Kingdom of God', I asked Rod what those words meant and he explained to me I needed to be baptised so that my sins will be washed away and I will be born again as a new person, that is a child of Christ. Well, I took a while to think about it but I did take it seriously in my heart.

On the 28th February 2003, God sent another message that I read, Isaiah 54:17. I didn't say much, when the time was up I went home and read the Scripture. It says:

'No weapon formed against you shall prosper, and every tongue which rises against you in judgement you shall condemn. This is the heritage of the servants of the Lord, and their righteousness is from Me, Says the Lord.'

This was another Scripture that was sent to me only 4 days from the day I was asked to read the whole Chapter in John 3. I noticed the Scripture was to do with my protection, sent by God Himself, and since I came to know who He is I believed what He said. It is obvious He understood the fear that was in me when I thought of approaching my family, so by this Scripture He convinced me He was aware of it and He will be there for me against any weapon that would be formed against me. Then I also remembered when He once verbally told me 'I will protect you'.

CHAPTER 7

MY BAPTISM

As days went by I reckoned the truth that was locked in my heart, so I made up my mind and prepared to tell Rod I was ready to be baptised. I aimed to tell him the first time he came into the Centre again. It didn't take him long, one day, out of the blue and at his usual time, I saw him wandering round the Centre and coming towards my classroom. He said he just came in to say hello and of course being a local man he knew many people around. Knowing he does not come in for nothing, I wanted to be the first one to surprise him that day and as my heart was pumping fast I was keen to break the news. The sun opposite my classroom was flashing bright rays towards me as if someone behind it was very excited, strangely I felt the same too. It felt like the bright rays were telling me go on, go on, so as Rod approached the room, I didn't let him settle for long before I said to him I have something to tell you.

So I confessed to Rod that I was ready for baptism. When he heard this he went in a shock, he didn't expect this from me and I knew for sure that he was shattered about the whole thing. In his mind I believe he thought he had done his job and was only waiting to see what would come out of it, perhaps the miracle of God, but he may not have expected it so soon. So he stood up mumbling in shock and excitement, and while in this state, he asked me, 'What did you say?' I replied to him, 'I said, I wanted to be baptised.' As he heard it again, he was a bit confused and started to walk round the room. I actually felt sorry for him seeing the way he was going round the room not knowing what to say. He was puzzled! But when he recovered he was happy and laughed out loud and eventually got his words back and said he will call his friend Peter and tell him about this so that they can make arrangements with the Church. But when I heard the name Peter, I remembered that one Peter I once had a go at him in the beginning of the whole process. I wasn't sure if he had to be there.

I wanted my baptism to be extremely private for these extreme reasons, I was born and bred as a Muslim and was about to convert to Christianity, a new faith and no one in my family had done it before or even knew about it. So I told Rod I only wanted to go with my friend, Miriam, the person I had nearly brought into Islam as I was going through my dialogues with Rod, but Rod reassured me that the event will take place in private and said it was good for Peter to be around with his wife because she will support me during the service. Having no idea about baptism I agreed with him because Peter's wife would be involved, even though I had never met her before, but I reminded him I only wanted my friend Miriam to be around me anywhere I would be in the Church. I realised then that Peter and his wife also worship at the same Church as Rod, so in this case Peter's wife would have more understanding of the Church services than Miriam, because she belonged to a different Church.

The appointment was then made on Wednesday, the 19th March 2003 at 7:30 pm at Rod's Church in Romford Road, East London. As I was still working at Broadwater Farm in Tottenham the appointment was set for after work on my way home. Before the actual date, my friend Miriam told me a little bit about what happens when someone gets baptised, so I had a rough idea of what to expect and what to carry with me when we went there. She told me to bring in some spare clothes as baptism involves going in the water so my body will be wet. As a matter of fact it didn't seem convincing to me when it comes to getting wet and changing but she told me about the changing rooms in the Church especially sorted for these services. So the time came and after work Rod hired a cab to take us to the Church. On the way, I saw a cluster of stars in the sky alongside the moon, that day it was a crescent moon with that usual bright star very close to it, a cluster of stars were beside them all moving towards the same direction as we were. I observed this all the way to the Church and when we got there I looked up and saw the moon and all the stars waited above the roof of the Church on the sky. I kept quiet, I did not tell Rod or anyone else about it.

When we entered the Church I saw a few people inside it so I became anxious and cautiously reminded Rod about my privacy. He said these people would normally take a video of anyone who is getting baptised as a routine so that they can show the person when it is all over but he told me not to worry and everything will be OK. The video will not be shown in public. I took his word on that. So with my friend Miriam beside me, Peter's wife showed us the room deep inside the Church for me to change and prepare for the service. Miriam helped me out in everything and insisted I held on tight to my clothes as I go down the water as they might get lift up. This was the last straw to me, it was the last thing I would want to hear, and it made me very nervous even though she had already cautioned me about this before-hand. So I made sure I had something comfortable on me as I sank in the water.

As soon as I finished changing, we were taken to this place at the back room where I found a very wide bathroom filled with water. Rod asked if the water was ready and introduced me to his Pastor who was in charge of that water and the whole thing. There were seven people in the room in total including Rod, Peter and his wife and Miriam, my friend. I was the eighth person in the group, so these seven people were my witnesses. They all stood in a circle facing the water and I was standing beside the Pastor. After the introduction, the Pastor looked at me and asked, 'What is your testimony?', 'Why are you becoming a Christian? 'What has God done to you?' I opened my mouth and started to speak about my experiences; I tried to be brief and so I only gave a summary of the revelations but not in detail. As soon as I finished I saw everyone praying and while doing this, some knelt down bending their knees and some prostrated lying flat on the floor. I saw one gentleman prostrating flat on the floor and Rod knelt down and kept prostrating. I heard the voice of Peter's wife saying, 'You are the chosen one' and suddenly I heard them all speaking in a different language. As this was happening, I suddenly felt my knees going down and the Pastor asked me what was the matter?, I said, 'I don't know, my knees are going down'; and as my knees went down by themselves my whole body eventually went down, so I laid down on the floor but was fully conscious. As I was lying down on the floor those people kept praying, their voices went a bit louder as they prayed in this peculiar language I now know is called 'tongues'. Despite that I was fully conscious I could not stand up straight away, a few minutes later I stood up and the Pastor asked if I was ready to go into the water. I said I was, so he explained to me what he was going to do and asked me if I agree to be baptised in the name of Jesus. I said, 'Yes' and confessed I am a sinner and accepted the Lord Jesus to be my Lord and Saviour. Then the Pastor sent me into the water. I remembered to hold on tight on my clothes as I went in face up.

I was about a few minutes in that water and I didn't feel scared. In fact, even though I was in the water for a few minutes, it felt like I was far away from that place and did not even hear anyone speaking, it was so peaceful. As I was lifted up from the water, the first thing I checked was my clothes and was pleased to see everything was in place and stuck on my body, they did not get lifted up! When it was all over, I was welcomed to the Kingdom of God, and one gentleman asked me if I could bring in some people who may wish to be saved, I said, 'Yes, I will'. He asked me do you know roughly how many? I said, '2 billion.' He was surprised and stared at me, but kept quiet.

We then walked outside the room into the main area and there I was shown the clips of my baptism and was rest assured they will not be made public. They kept their word because I've never heard anything spoken about it to this day. This was a memorable day to me, it was like my birth day, I was full of joy when I walked out of that Church and outside it I was welcomed by my usual, the cluster of stars and that bright star alongside the moon were waiting above the roof of the Church as the service went on; and on my way home the moon was left alone but expanded to a very large size indeed and moved alongside us as we drove home. This time I decided to show it to my friends and said, 'God is very happy, today the moon is extremely large and beautiful.' It was in golden colour. When my friends went on their way, the moon accompanied me all the way home and waited in its usual places in the sky. I remember this day as my birthday, actually even more than that because I was born again today! And by the blood of Jesus I am made 'holy' and 'righteous', how wonderful! I believe this is the only blood that can wash away the sin of men and make someone holy and righteous in front of God. There is no sacrifice other than this. It was all done on that cross.

I got home late that day, and one of my little ones said to me, 'Mum you are late today', I said, 'Yes, I was very busy today, but I am home now.' I didn't realise that she had actually gone into my bag and found some wet clothes, but she kept it to herself. Years later as I wrote this book she told me she thought I went swimming that day.

Rod had actually completed his IT Course at the Centre after my baptism but hanged on around the place and visited every week for over a year. He would be around me any time I needed him but even though I hadn't asked for him he would still be around. Anyway, he only lived two streets away from the Centre. He was like a carer for me. Soon after my baptism, he came to see me and warned that I was not exempt from tribulations. At first I didn't understand it so he explained that even though I was saved, I was not exempt from tribulations; he said we all go through tribulations in life. Well, I said okay, I understand. Months later he tried to encourage me to go to his Church but this was a bit difficult for me because I lived far away.

CHAPTER 8

THE BOTTOMLESS PIT

Sometime later he came to me and said Salma the Lord is going to take you to the 'Bottomless Pit!' I looked at him in shock and said, 'What?' He repeated that the Lord said He is going to take me to the Bottomless Pit! Well, thinking that I've just been saved this was more than a shock to me. So I said, 'But I don't want to go there'. He knew that I was scared so he explained it better and said, 'no, He is only going to take you there to see the place, you are not going to stay there.' I was relieved then and said, 'Oh, OK then.' After this message, I carried on with my daily work but actually started to read the Bible.

Time passed and this conversation about the bottomless pit was out of my mind when I had a dream never to be forgotten. I found myself in a place below the earth full of sharp and slippery rocks everywhere I touched. The place was below ground level, in a pit with wet slippery rocks very dangerous to climb on. I did not like the place at all and in my dream I was struggling to come out of it, so I was climbing up from the bottom holding onto these filthy slippery rocks. It was really scary because if I fell down I knew I wouldn't come out in one piece, I could have broken every part of my body. Thankfully I didn't fall and despite the struggle I managed to climb out to the open space and stand on the ground. When I was standing on the ground, I looked back into the pit and saw a depth of darkness covered with rocks. The visibility was very low down there but it was possible to see my way round.

I was so glad I was out of the pit and so I started walking on the foot path until I came to a place where I decided to take some rest. I sat down on a place just above a tiny pit most likely to have been dug by somebody and hanged my legs over, I could easily step in and out of it. The colour of the soil inside the pit was reddish brown. Anyway, not long after I decided to rest there I saw someone I knew walking towards me, he was a very famous person in the world. He actually came to me so I said hello to him mentioning his name. He said hello and sat down with me for a while then he went away. I saw him walking towards the place I had been, the pit, and the whole surrounding seemed very familiar to him. He walked as if he knew the whole place very well.

I watched him going away but as I turned my head back I saw someone else standing next to the little pit where I was resting. For some reasons I knew his name so I said, 'Hello Michael.' He replied, 'Hello Salma, I've come to take you home.' This person was also tall, of whitish olive complexion and wearing a long greyish green coat, a kind of a detective style coat. I said thanks and held his hand, and as soon as I held his hand he took me out of the little pit and I was out of the area, it happened very fast, as if flying, then the dream ended. When I woke up I first made sure I was in my own bed. The bottomless pit is not a place for anyone to be, by all means please don't be there! I then told this dream to Rod just to let him know that the event had taken place.

CHAPTER 9

A VISIT TO HEAVEN

Again within the same year, Rod came to me with another message he had received from the Lord. This message was about God taking me to heaven and the dream started this way:

I was somewhere in the countryside in a kind of a village but not in the UK. I saw some people around the area just carrying on with their normal lives. It happened in the day time when I was walking around the area with my two children when I suddenly saw myself going up in the air carrying my children on both sides. I went up (with no wings) and as soon as that happened my hands were stretched up towards the sky and from that moment I did not notice my children. I went far up in the air and as I approached this huge long gate standing in the air I heard the voice saying, 'And the gate will open.' As the voice said these words the gate opened at the same time. This gate was very tall in height and curved on both sides at the top. Compared to the size of this gate, I was like a little bird flying through it and I entered this vast place while still on the air. The place was vast and very beautiful and even though I didn't see anyone in there I naturally asked, 'What is the weather in here?' And the voice said, 'Spring.'

This particular voice however was deep, similar to the one I once heard laughing loud from my heart, from inside me, after I teased the Lord on one particular occasion when I was trying to demonstrate to my son how the Lord works on His lights through me. But on that particular occasion the Lord tested my faith by delaying to show the light I had asked for while my son was waiting for it as we drove home. So because of His delay I started to get really worried but I kept calm, I didn't want to be noticed; and while in that state the Lord eventually revealed where the moon was so I was able to prove it to my son. From this day I discovered that the Lord has sense of humour and as I was relieved that I was eventually able to prove to my son what I had told him about the moon, I decided to tease the Lord back in return, so I said something to Him in my heart that really got Him laughing really loud inside me, I could even feel it, let alone hear it loud and clear; so this is how I remembered that similar voice once again when He said 'Spring.'

I entered the gate like a little tiny bird flying into a different atmosphere. Compared to the size of the gate I looked really tiny as I approached it, and once I entered it my clothes changed to a beautiful outfit in pure white and my head glowed like the sun. I could see myself so beautiful and covered with light, I was singing as I was flying and diving in the air. To begin with I was just flying beside the gate in this vast beautiful place, I was singing and playing in the air, stretching my arms and diving, I was full of joy and displayed my happiness in the air. After a while I moved on to see the rest of the place and as I continued flying I looked down and saw lines of beautiful pinkish white blossoms in the whole area as far as I could see. It was a very beautiful place indeed; I couldn't see the end of it.

As I was still there, I suddenly found myself inside this kind of mansion, a church like house on the right hand side of the gate as you enter it. This is when I noticed my two little children back with me again. This house was a kind of a mansion or a Church but had no light in it, there were no decorations or furniture inside it either. It was like a place that was left empty for a long time. After walking through it, I sat down with my little children for a while and then walked outside and sat in front of the main door. As I sat down there I looked towards the gate I had entered through and suddenly saw two people, a man and a woman, walking towards me as if coming from the same gate. Surprisingly, they were my brother and his wife walking towards me, and as they came closer, they looked worn out and tired. I saw some parts of their skin burnt out and turned dark. Their arms and faces were burnt and turned very dark as if burnt in a fire. My brother's hair, which is usually loose curls, had turned thick and stood up hard like screws on his head. When they met me, the first thing they said was they were sorry for all they had done to me. I said to them it is okay and asked them where they had been. They said they had been in the war and said 'Iran is burning down there.' I felt sorry for them and was hurt to see them like that; then the dream ended.

CHAPTER 10

TRIBULATIONS

Time passed and Rod was at the door for a visit, nothing strange, just his normal routine. This day he said to me, 'Salma there is a devil around you who wants to kill you, but he can't get to you personally so he will go into the ones nearer to you to destroy you.' I said to him, 'the devil wants to kill me?' He said, 'Yes, he does, but because he can't get into you he will go into the ones nearer to you, to destroy you.' So this was the beginning of the tribulations in my new life as a Christian, a believer in Christ.

Demonic interventions
Several months later after receiving that horrendous message, I started to go through certain experiences that had never happened in my life before. It all started with my older daughter, the 13 year old who was living her life as a normal child and all of a sudden she was possessed by a demon and got me into tremendous difficulties. She started by acting strangely and becoming out of order, sometimes screaming out loud or laughing and sometimes being very sick lying flat on the floor. There were times I thought I would lose her. In fact, anyone could tell that something was wrong in her and from this point things were not normal any more. I then remembered what Rod had told me about the devil who wanted to kill me but because it couldn't get into me it would go into anyone nearer me to destroy me. I knew then this was it so I told Rod about it as soon as it started. There

were times that the demon would come into my daughter and make her really sick causing a concern to everyone. It was frightening the way it possessed her, making her sick and screaming loud. These episodes would take long hours and my daughter would be extremely tired when it was all over; she would then remain in anxiety thinking about when it will come back to her again! It wasn't happening everyday though, it was occasional but most of the time it would choose the time when I was all alone with my younger daughter in the house. It would come when there would be no other adults to help me. It was as if it was choosing the best times to possess her so it could put me on the spot not knowing what to do on my own. My younger daughter was only 10 at that time, too young to understand what was going on.

Although Rod was very supportive in prayers on the phone, he was stranded at home because of a very long distance to where I lived. So he thought it would be even better if I took the child with me to my work place so he could pray for her after the lessons. So we agreed on the days that I would bring her for prayers from time to time. On one occasion when Rod was praying for her the demon in her got really serious and grabbed Rod, a 14 stone gentleman and threw him into the corner; anyway, Rod got up and we continued praying, however, the noise attracted the neighbour's attention, who was working late in her office that day, so she popped in to see what was happening. She was a Christian herself so she immediately understood it was a demon on board and decided to join in the prayer, she also advised us to take the girl to Church to get prayed for. She left after a while and Rod and I continued to pray until it released her. That day it took longer than usual and my daughter was extremely tired when it was all over, after all she was only a kid. When Rod was lifted over and thrown away by the demon, he was amazed and asked how can a 13 year old girl lift up and throw away a 14 stone man? He said he hadn't seen that before.

As the episodes continued they wore all of us out. The

difficulties added up with my job responsibilities and looking after my family at home. It then went on from being possessed at home to being targeted at any place any time, but I thank God that it never happened in the streets or at school or when she was alone. There was one time when I didn't know what to do, I could not reach Rod on the phone for advice when the demon struck her, so being desperate I decided to take my child to the Church where I had been baptised. So I drove to Church with her and my younger daughter but I could not find it and decided to return home. On my way home I was trying to hide my tears from my young one as I didn't want her to be frightened. We managed to get home safely and eventually managed to contact Rod by phone. I told him the whole story that I even tried to get to Church but could not find it. He straight away phoned the other Pastor that he knew in Deptford, as this place is also in the South East of London it would be more or less nearer to our home; but the Pastor agreed to wait for us at that Church instead. As it was already getting late in the night I could not go there with the children, I didn't even know where the Church was and there were no SatNavs at that time. For Rod also, living miles away in North London, it was difficult for him to make it to our house in the day let alone in the night. So it was a kind of a 'Catch 22' situation, the devil had it set up at his best. Then the Pastor in Deptford Church asked me if I believed in Jesus Christ and if I was baptised, I said yes I was, then he told me to read Psalm 91, a prayer for protection day and night every day, and he will also pray for us. I thanked him and trusted in God. That night my children and I all slept on my bed in my bedroom.

The next day, the demon told my daughter he was going to bring many other demons to come to us over night. I was really frightened by this but I trusted in God, and when the night came I took my children to bed with me in my bedroom as they were all scared of what was going to happen. I could not sleep that night, I stayed awake and prayed, reading Psalm 91 and trusted in God for our protection. So as the demon said it would bring many others with him that night, I felt something very strange happening around mid-night when the children were fast asleep. I was half awake when I saw a figure of someone tall and thin walking round our bed a few times and then stood up still in front of me not far from the bed. As He stood up there looking at me, I saw my body lifting itself up and prostrating towards Him; yes, my body just did it by itself, I then lifted up my face and stretched my hands towards Him trying to hold Him but He walked back slightly so I couldn't touch Him. After a while He disappeared and I turned back to sleep. It eventually turned out to be a very peaceful night instead.

On one other occasion my daughter was possessed in front of her brother and sister-in-law when they came over for a visit, and the demon said it would harass them, severely threatening to harm them, but thank God it had never happened. With constant prayers day and night, the situation slowed down and eventually eased, but the truth of the matter was we were all shaken up. As the situations eased up I was sent a Scripture from the Gospel of Matthew, talking about when demons leave the body of the person they had previously possessed and how they can return seven times stronger than they were the first time they came into the body. So Rod advised me to think about getting the children baptised as well. I thought it would be a good idea, so when they were about 11 and 14 I took them to Church to be baptised. However, the older daughter, the one who had been possessed by a demon, did not agree with idea of going into the water, she seemed so scared at first and when she eventually did, she seemed disturbed half way round and came out of it; and as this had to come from someone's heart she was left alone, she was not forced to go into the water. The younger one went in fully, though at that time they were both young and did not actually understand what baptism really meant. In fact, we were all trying to understand our new faith, a major change in our lives.

Tribulation in the marriage

After a long time living as a single mother I decided to re-marry, 6 years after the divorce from my previous husband, the father of my two daughters. So I went home and got married in Tanzania in 2001; and in July 2003 my new husband finally came to England to join me and the children, after two years of battling for his visa, so he was finally allowed to come and settle with us in England. We were all Muslims when we got married in 2001 but despite the painful waiting of two years, the cost I incurred and the time and effort I had put in dealing with his case, this man had only one thing in mind, which I failed to notice from the beginning, until I found out this was his opportunity to sort out his life and his family abroad. This is what I came to understand half way through our lives together.

To cut a long story short, I thought I was made up in my marriage this time, I thought I wasn't risking much because I was introduced to him by my best friend, the aunt of my first two sons, who had been married to his own brother for many years, so he is basically a brother-in-law to my best friend. So to me I thought I'd got it right this time and my children will grow up with a father, but it didn't turn out to be that way. The stress and difficulty I went through for sorting him out was immense and it wasn't just sorting out his settlement visa, it was also to do with everything else that applied to him when living this country. Things like job applications, national insurance number, bank account etc. to name a few, as he was rightly permitted to live in the country as a UK resident. The cost I suffered included the Barrister's cost, on top of the monthly costs I was paying the lawyers for two years before the Court hearing; and even though I had a reasonable salary coming in each month I had to take out a loan to accommodate all these expenses; though I admit as soon as he secured a job he contributed something towards the loan and he also took out a new car for us on finance and paid it in full, therefore in some ways he helped out with the costs.

But as soon as he came in the country it didn't take me

long to start wondering if I had made the right decision, I started discovering his true colours just six months after we had started to live together. To name the least, I went through bad attitudes and regular insults, there were persistent disappointments, mourning, lowering my self-esteem, listening to distant relatives more than me, honouring male and female friends more than me and seeing himself younger than me when in fact he was a year older than me, which generated the feeling of being uncomfortable with me when we went out together or in gatherings. These things and much more made me worried so they triggered my thoughts about his real intentions. Most of the time he would use phrases like he was only here as a passer-by, which meant he might be with us one day and the next day he would be gone; he would say this to me in front of the family. I wonder why I failed to take it seriously after various reminders. Perhaps because I was truthful to him when I took my vows and because in my mind I thought I had married a man to spend the rest of my life together and to be a father to my children. I also remembered his own confession about his previous marriage; he told me he went through tremendous difficulties in his previous two marriages and has had enough, he now wanted to settle down, so I believed him. He was also a father of two young girls and as I was also a mother of two young children I thought we had much in common. So having this background together I believed my married life was eventually sorted – but I should have known better. I even failed to realise he was setting up the time to leave me in a coded phrase he used when he was talking to his parents on the phone; he would always tell them he knew what he was doing. What a shame, I didn't understand and as life went on I kept thinking his attitudes would change but it was a great mistake.

He continued his unreasonable behaviour and mental cruelty towards me to accomplish his mission. He would be insulting me and lie to me, hoping that I would eventually give up and ask him to leave. He once told me people would have to see me bad not him, so they would see I was the one who threw him out of the house. To support this lie, he once agreed with me to go on a business trip to Dubai to see if we could start a business there, but as soon as I got there he twisted up the whole thing and accused me of being unfaithful to him. He said he was convinced that I went to Dubai to meet with my ex-husband, the one who lives in Oman, the father of my sons, instead of what we had both planned and agreed together, because I had missed one of his phone calls. He pressed these accusations on me despite it being that my son, who came to collect me from the airport, was the one who picked up the phone and spoke to him as we were just coming out of the car at my uncle's house where I was going to stay. So tired from a long journey, I told my son to tell him I have just arrived and was fine but was in the middle of sorting out the luggage from the car and would speak to him tomorrow as soon as I had sorted the telephone SIM card. My son told him just that but he didn't want to believe it was the case, he did not believe him nor trusted me or my relatives with whom I was staying. Instead, he accused me of meeting with my ex-husband, my son's father, from whom I had been divorced from a long time ago and who I had not seen for many years. So he exaggerated these false accusations to his parents and some of my relatives, so that I would be proven unfaithful and hence, suiting his plans that I would be seen as unfaithful wife, he could make his way out.

When I got home from abroad, I tried to prove to him I was innocent but it was to no avail. Instead he twisted it and told me he had forgiven me, which hurt my feelings and made me really upset because I hadn't done anything wrong to be forgiven for, it was mental cruelty, he was psychologically assaulting me. I said to him, 'You don't need to forgive me for this because I haven't done anything against you, if I did I would be grateful'. This man left me with this scar for a very long time, but I have now forgiven him from my heart. Anyway, after this accusation I remembered some of the stories he had once told me about his past relationships, that he had caught his ladies with other men before, which might have triggered his feelings when I went abroad; but having experienced this, I was just not sure whether the accusations about his previous wives were true or actually framed just like mine. However, I once again tried to give it time in the hope that he would change attitudes but in reality I wasn't doing myself any good. He also tried to win my children by poisoning my relationship with them, because he would be good to them when I was at work telling them I was always miserable with them and shouted at them when I returned home, expecting them to believe him because they were young, but at the same time he would be miserable to them and constantly accusing them when I was home with them. He knew what he was doing so he didn't care much that these children would be questioning themselves as to why they would be good children when mum was at work and be bad when she was home with them. So as time went by the whole family was affected by his behaviour, it wasn't doing any good to any of us, especially to my children.

His mission was accomplished when my 16 year old daughter came home late one night and his reactions made my older daughter shout at him, thinking he was going to attack her sister. Watching him grabbing her sister's hair and pulling her around she yelled at him and told him to leave the house. This concluded his mission and even though these words did not come out from my mouth, he didn't take it that way, it was the end of it all. He called his friend straight away that night to come and pick him up from the house. He had no need of talking to me about the situation so in the same night he gathered his stuff and went in the van with his friend. He also used my own cousin to find him a rented property using the reason that my daughter threw him out of the house. My cousin did not live far from us so he found him a flat near his area. It was all over! He separated from me in May 2009 and three months later at the end of August, after 6 years of living together and 8 years of marriage, I faced another divorce. He left me with a 4 year old daughter. The little one prophesied by Rod.

Bankruptcy

The tribulations continued and did not exclude the 'Bankruptcy' because as a result of losing my full time job I could not keep up with the bills and the interest on loan started to build on. Things started to get harder when I took up my maternity leave from work in 2004, my contract was ended before my return to work as the Centre lost its contract with the main College; and although a year later I managed to find a part time employment from the main College (CONEL), the hours I managed to get were not enough to accommodate the living expenses and the loan I had previously taken. My rent arrears were also accumulating and eventually I could not cope with all the pressures, so I decided to follow the instructions from the chain of horrible letters I was receiving from the companies, which was to seek legal advice as they intended to declare me 'bankrupt'. I suffered aggressive letters nonstop coming from all sides almost every day chasing me for the money, followed by numerous phone calls from early mornings to late evenings. My soul was not at rest.

The financial difficulties were also part of the tribulations within the marriage as the one income from the husband while I was on maternity leave was not enough to settle everything down. The situations were too much for me to cope with and I thank God for keeping me still, but when enough was enough I made up my mind to seek advice from the Citizens Advice Bureau as advised in those horrendous letters. However, when I decided to go through this I had to go through everything all alone, I didn't get even moral support from my husband. So I took a step out and went but at first I landed at the wrong place so I had to be directed back to a different place, which thank God happened to be near my home. There I met a gentleman who was polite and professional in his job, he explained to me what bankruptcy involves and the best way I could take the matter forward. He told me there were two ways of sorting the problem out, either by declaring myself bankrupt or let the companies do it for me. He said that was the way forward for my best interest. I measured his thoughts and saw no other way so I declared it myself. The man helped me with the forms and explained all the procedures including the investigations and what to expect at Court. So I went through it alone, the husband did not come with me at Court, he said it was not a matter for him to come because I was not being prosecuted.

But was I alone? No, I was with my God, I saw His signal through the Court window! He was there with me, my Heavenly Father, and when I saw His signal I gained strength at least good enough to face the Judge, the last person I would ever wanted to see, meeting him face to face was my worst nightmare! But it wasn't only me who felt that way, I noticed a young woman in the waiting area, who at least had a shoulder to lean on as she had her mother near her but thinking it through she decided to give up and went home, she could not face the judge. I said to myself, 'at least she has her mother with her,' but despite her comfort the young woman could not face it, she was full of fear. Well, my own shaking eased up and while in the Judge's Chamber I looked through the window on my right side just to make sure. The Judge did not ask me much but wanted me to confirm that I would not borrow anything more than what he had told me that day, so he asked me to confirm if I understood that and I did. He also said if they didn't find any problems in their investigations I would be discharged within 6 months, which eased up the tension even though I was still worried. I looked at him and said thank you; then gentle tears started drawing down my face as I left the room. I went back to the waiting room and saw other people who'd just faced their fate like me, and when my turn was up I was called in and informed of what to expect, just as what that gentleman said at the Citizen's Advice Bureau. In the same year 6 months later, I received a letter from the Court explaining that they didn't find any problems in their investigations therefore I was discharged, I was given un-conditional discharge! Since then I have never taken another loan no matter how small it is. I have lived my life without even credit cards nor have I taken any store cards anymore. I just work and live a simple life with my family.

Going bankrupt is not a place to be, even though it is a

way of overcoming financial debt I suggest it should not be taken as safe haven, it should only be considered as a last resort. There is a lot more that someone could be put through then just overcoming their debt; there is more than just losing a Bank account and credit cards. The feeling of being investigated and disconnected from ordinary life style in a modern society is like being disconnected from the system and blocked out from the advantages in a society for long time. When it comes to even being prohibited the right to open a new account until the whole case is over puts someone in an uncomfortable position in a modern society; and although some Banks may agree to offer a simple cash account the services are very limited so you would be still locked out. In the worst case scenario it could lead to enforcement if the case is not genuine. On the other hand, however, it can still be a last resort that can help innocent people who would get into financial difficulties unwillingly, so it is a kind of generosity if used in genuine conditions.

Car failure

However, in October 2009, just two months after the divorce, my car broke down with engine failure, so things got even harder, it was even difficult for me to get to work let alone going to Church. This was supposed to be that new car that my husband bought on finance which came with the agreement cover for 4 years. We bought the car in 2005, surprisingly as soon as the agreement was over the engine broke down; and as the car was supposed to be new, it was hard to find the used spare parts of its kind and the new part would cost a fortune. When I took it to the garage I was told the cost for repairing it would be about £900 for the new parts before labour; and with the financial difficulties I was going through at the time, this was a lot of money to come from me, so the car remained at the garage for a long time and has never got sorted out. Well, that was it, after the divorce came a problem with the car, so I was left to use public transport to get to work for a long time, from the South East to East London almost every day.

On the 30th September 2003, Rod came in with a message saying, 'You've got the light of the Holy Spirit around you now, the Lord knows what you are going through.' I didn't say much about it I just accepted the message and moved on but I felt at least God was aware of my tough times.

CHAPTER 11

JEHOVAH JERRAH

Several weeks later after Rod's message, I made an attempt to visit a small Church in my local area slightly away from where I lived. As I could not have faced my husband and told him I was going to Church, the distance from home to this Church was just right for such manoeuvres, after all I was only going to Church.

This Church was very small, it was more like a little Chapel in the street compared to the one I was baptised into. I didn't know anyone in that Church I only went there for worship; so I made my way in and sat down. I noticed some people staring at me probably wondering who I was but it was obvious that I didn't know how to worship yet or how to pray but I carried on following what they did, so I stood up whey they did and sat down as they sat down. However, as we were worshipping I suddenly heard the word 'Jehovah' and all the prayers and worship were then directed to Him, we were made to stand up for a while as this was practiced. Well, I was new to the Christian faith and did not have much knowledge of how they worshipped so I wondered who this Jehovah was, as since the beginning of my experiences I had never heard about this name, I only knew about Jesus. Because of this I became seriously frustrated and angry and thought those people might be worshipping a different God, so I picked up my bag and walked out straight away.

I drove home frustrated and as usual the sun accompanied me home. I was still angry and as I approached my garage still upset, I looked up towards the sun and asked God, 'Who is Jehovah?' The sun flashed at me immediately as a response, so I asked Him again, 'Are you going to tell me who Jehovah is?' The sun flashed at me once again, so I said 'OK.' I must admit I was very upset that day and apparently did not want any confusion in my life, so I was angry when I asked those questions. I'm sure the Lord understood it so He reflected through the sun. That day I had also noticed different reactions in the display of the moon, as the Lord also uses these objects as a means of communication with me. I do feel His presence when these objects follow me. So when the sun flashed back to me after my second question, I knew He was going to let me know but I didn't know when or how He was going to do it.

Well, on the 12th November 2003, I saw Rod wondering round the stairs at work talking to other people, I knew he rarely comes in empty. I must admit I didn't know what it was all about but I did hear Rod a kind of complaining from a distance somewhere in the building, speaking to himself, 'why me, why me,' before he finally came and see me. He was a kind of uncomfortable. When he eventually came to me this time he told me, 'Salma the Lord wants to speak to you.' I was surprised to hear this, so I asked him, 'Do you mean the Lord wants to speak to me?' Well, there was no point of rebelling, I was just surprised! This was totally odd and new to me but I said OK. He told me to follow him in the small office downstairs and the Lord will speak to me there. This was really strange and suspicious. He then said to me, 'Salma the Lord will speak through me.' For this I didn't keep quiet; I asked him 'Rod are you saying that the Lord will speak through you?' He said, 'Yes.' I told him that was really strange and I wasn't actually comfortable about it. I started saying in my heart God does not go into people and speak through them, this is demonic!

Anyway, I agreed to go downstairs with my friend Miriam and when we got there he asked us to sit on the chairs near him so he was sitting opposite us. Rod started to speak things about Miriam that weren't unusual but I suddenly saw

Miriam's knees bending down and she remained knelt down until Rod finished speaking about her. The other difference that day was that Rod's voice was not normal, it wasn't fully his own voice. When Miriam eventually got up she was told to go, so I was left alone with Rod ready to speak to me. To be honest, I didn't tell him about this but I believed the whole thing was demonic and felt like leaving the place straight away; but I didn't want to disappoint him. I am sure he could read it from my face.

Rod looked at me and knew that I doubted him; anyway he gently shut the door, sat down and started speaking to me. As he spoke, his voice was deeper than normal and as he continued it sounded like thunder at one point when he mentioned the name 'Jehovah Jerrah'. I actually trembled at this point and felt some reactions on my knees, but I remained stubborn and hid my feelings very well. By now I had known Rod for a long time since he enrolled at the Centre so I could confirm that it wasn't his voice at all at that time! So he attracted my attention I wanted to discover some more. When he started speaking, he started with these words:

'I am He, I am He
I am the One
I am Jehovah Jerrah
You want to glorify Me, my child
No weapon formed against you shall prosper
You have work to do, my child
You will go through nations and spread My Word
I love you, for I am love
Your family will be saved
Walk through Me, do not walk through men, for men will
lead you astray
Do not fear who will persecute you, for they persecuted Me
when I came here on earth in flesh
I shine My light through you everywhere you go,
for I am Light
I will send you a Helper
I will protect you

You will be blessed, both physically and spiritually
Do not worry about Mahfoodh, for he is searching
Do not worry about your husband, I know his heart
I love you, my child
My beautiful, beautiful child, I love you. I love you'

Then the voice faded away. This message came to me not long from the day I questioned the Lord about Jehovah, something that I had only kept to myself, I had never told Rod about it. I was wondering then how did Rod come to know about the 'Jehovah' issue. So since this episode I was left with a question mark as to whether God could really go into someone and speak through them, because I thought of it as demonic and especially because as far as I could remember throughout my childhood experiences I had witnessed demons going into people's lives and either wreck them or settle in them. I had witnessed demons speaking through people even in my own family and some relatives, and especially when one was sent to kill me as a young adult, so to me demons were not strangers. In the lives of many people where I came from, so as much as I know, they could come into anyone and even make their homes in them.

Going back to the point however, Rod did not know about my business with God about Jehovah and when he started talking he spoke in the first person, saying, 'I am He, I am He, I am the One', so I began to wonder; and I could not deny that I trembled when his voice once sounded like thunder when he mentioned the name 'Jehovah Jerrah'. In as much as I hid my feelings very well, Rod looked me in the eye knowing how I felt but made it as if he didn't notice anything and continued to speak. To be honest with you, I have lived with this doubt for a very long time but at the same time I also knew that I was all alone when I asked God to explain to me about Jehovah, so on the other hand I could not deny that it was Jesus who spoke to me that day, first because I was the one who asked Him who Jehovah was and all alone, second, when He was confirming to me about who He is in His statements, and thirdly, He was speaking in the first person. 'So could Rod really take the role of Jesus?', I asked myself. By these responses I knew that Rod could not have made it up, it should have been Jesus Himself which meant that that day Jesus came down Himself to answer my question through Rod. May God bless him.

That day the Lord also confirmed that He is the One who shines light through me everywhere I go, and even said that He Himself is Light. Now referring back to this after a while I felt how wonderful it is to know Jesus, thinking that He is God but through His love He could bring Himself down to the lowest to reach us. I thought of all other revelations He had done and displayed vividly to me, I thought of all the messages and Scriptures He had sent me and what He said He would do came to pass. When He said that He would show me it was Him He proved it by miracles and wonders through His lights and Personal interventions. So as He had initially said, He first opened my eyes through Scriptures then used His lights to connect to me; and in that particular conversation that day, He actually confirmed that He is the One who shines light through me everywhere I go. I said to myself, 'how could Rod make all this up?'

Everything that Rod said confirmed that God hears me and knows everything about me and my family. When he said I should not worry about my son because he is searching I said nothing but when it was over I wished I had asked Him if my son would eventually find him; but I then realised that my answer was already there, the Lord did say that day that my family will be saved; so I believe in His word. Now the issue about my husband was also amazing, the Lord said I should not worry about him, He knew his heart. How can a normal person read another person's heart? It was impossible that Rod could do it himself. Anyway, maybe if I hadn't been doubtful I might have had a chance to ask some questions but now I just wish He had told me.

God also knew about my little plan all the way back to when I was a Muslim but He wanted me to know Him first. When He said, 'You want to glorify Me, my child' I remembered what I said in my heart a long time ago that I only wanted to work for God when I reached the age of forty, and in these right times He came forward and revealed Himself to me and made His purpose known to me. He gradually started working in me in 2002 and a year later in 2003 He made Himself known to me and told me I have work to do, and that is 'to teach His Word through nations'. From this message I understood that that was my 'Call', the purpose that God had for me. He told me to walk through Him and not to fear those who will persecute me, He locked His message with His love and protection and said He will protect me, He will send me a Helper and no weapon formed against me shall prosper. He called me His beautiful child. Since then, it has been about 10 years since I received my call to serve the Lord but I haven't done much. May be it was my preparation time.

After a series of tribulations, one on top of the other, I discussed the issues with one of the female Pastors at Church. She talked to the Senior Pastor and they arranged for me and my family to have a special prayer meeting at the Church; so one day my children and I went Church for this special prayer of 'forgiveness'. In fact, it was a very sensitive and lengthy prayer led by the two Pastors from the Church. It wasn't all peaceful during the prayer because one of my daughters who was once possessed by a demon suddenly started screaming at her loudest and the situation got me and the other daughter really worried, thinking that the demon was returning to her. Thank God there were more people that day and they were Pastors so with intensive prayers the screaming ended on the same day. When the prayer was finished, the Pastors suggested another appointment for a second prayer, but this was to pray for us and for the house, so it was going to be a home visit.

On 13th November 2009, soon after the prayer of forgiveness the Pastors came to our house for the second prayer. The people who came over were a team of three Pastors and one Intercessor and even though they went through tremendous difficulty in finding our house they eventually managed to get there. Surprisingly enough on this same day I was also stranded myself from getting home on time when the road was going to be closed because of a sudden accident which happened on my way home from the Town Centre; fortunately my bus was the last one allowed to get through.

The three Pastors divided their portions in the house, one for each floor, they prayed throughout house, in every room on all floors including the box rooms on the ground floor, the garage and the patio. The whole house was covered with prayer and we were very grateful for their effort and care. When they had completed the house prayer, they all came to the living room and prayed for all of us holding hands in a circle. During the prayer my whole body once again went down by itself and I laid down flat on the floor, in the same way as it happened during my baptism; again I was awake and fully conscious, though I could not lift myself up straight away. They continued praying. At the end of the service, they told us to remove all the stuff that related to our previous faith and burn them; these were things like the Qur-an, text books, pictures, praying mats and any items related to Islam as their existence according to them could bring back the powers of the Islamic spirit. I agreed on that, as after all I didn't want to face anything worse than I had already faced. So sometime later I burnt all the books including all the Qur-an Books I had and threw away all the items associated to Islam that were in the house. After this there was much peace in us and our house except that I was still hurting from the divorce.

CHAPTER 12

PROPHECY OF A NEW CHILD

Sometime later after I found out about the Lord's purpose in me, Rod predicted my pregnancy and told me that he saw me in the skies wearing a white gown and carrying a child in my hands. As my husband was in the country, I thought it likely to happen and especially knowing Rod with his speeches. As usual I was surprised when I heard this but I just stared at him with my mouth open; I could not speak for a while. When I told my friend Miriam she didn't have much to say except staring at me and murmured 'Hmm.' A few months later I discovered I was really pregnant and when I told Rod about this he said prepare to paint the room in pink! I said, 'God bless this man!' Anyway, having two daughters already I thought I would have a little boy to close the womb but that was just a norm, I was full of joy. Strangely enough my friend Miriam also said she saw me on the skies with a little baby girl with curly hair. I just accepted it all and waited.

So the prophecy of my pregnancy also became true and as I continued working, Rod and Miriam helped me a lot without exhaustion, they even helped getting my lunch from the high street. They were like part of my family. Then the time came near the baby's birth when Rod came at lunch time and told me I will be on my own when I'm having the baby, my husband will not be there. He said it will be me and the Lord's Angels. I must admit I was disappointed that my husband wouldn't be there but I had to wait and see. When I was due and in labour I was taken to Queen Mary's Hospital to have my baby. In this pregnancy I went through 16 hours of labour before the baby came out, it was the longest pain I've ever had in all my pregnancies, and indeed as Rod had said, my husband was not there when the baby was born. He got frustrated because of the long wait but in his mind it was more important to do his job the next day, though he knew he was entitled to paternity leave if he wished to take it he decided not to. As he waited he even started insulting me while in pain, saying 'We have seen it all before', meaning he had been in the labour rooms with his previous wives before, so my pain was nothing strange to him. He then told me he was leaving so he wouldn't be late to work the next morning, I said to him 'okay,' even though I didn't feel good about it because I expected him to be there with me, but I didn't want to inject more pain into myself, I had labour pain to deal with. So he left the hospital and went home to sleep ready for work the next day.

When I was in labour, there was a midwife sitting close to me in the labour room. For some reason the midwife suddenly left the room and went somewhere and as the contraction ebbed away I saw a live vision of some men dressed up in green gowns like surgeons moving round the room working. As they moved around the room my eyes clashed directly with one of them, like the others he was busy walking around and then I heard the voices of the other ones talking with him. It all appeared all of a sudden in a blink of an eye so I didn't get what they were actually saying but I managed to get a close look of the one my eyes got clashed with. At that moment I actually remembered what Rod had told me about this but kept it to myself; and as soon as the vision was over, I started to push, and pushed hard; and my one sharp scream made the midwife to run in quickly and saw the little head popping out. She immediately called her partner saying, 'Come and see this!' Then the other one came in and saw a little head already popped up. It was a little girl, born at eight minutes to one in the morning. It was wonderful!

My experiences after confession and accepting Jesus as

my Lord and Saviour continued with a series of revelations and encounters, including dreams and visions as I was told they would but I was also told I was not exempt from tribulations.

CHAPTER 13

IN THE GOLDEN YACHT

Following the prophecy of my child, I had a particular dream out of many that I would also like to share. It was about me walking in the street in a particular country when I suddenly came up to a commotion. I had no idea why so many people were there but as I moved closer towards the middle of the commotion, I saw a group of about 40 men, all light skinned and dressed up in white gowns with white caps on their heads as if waiting for me. As I walked closer to them they all came to me and started walking ahead with me saying 'Illohi!, Illohi!'. As they said these words, they directed me along the street and walked with me until we entered into a door and came out to the other side of the place where there was only a sea in front of us. It was like an old port. As this was a dead end we stopped in a place not too far from where we first entered through the door. As I stood at this place I saw a 'Ship wreck' in the water standing still at the platform about ten metres away from where I was standing. Then I was motioned to step into the wreck and as I looked in it I saw two men standing on it. I stepped my right foot into the Ship and as I did this the Ship wreck suddenly turned into gold, all of it was gold. It was a very beautiful Yacht! So I was in the Yacht with these two men who were standing a little way behind me, I was standing near the front. The Yacht suddenly sped out into the sea; and as it took off, I enjoyed the sea view, it was like a celebration. I saw a lot of people standing beside the sea celebrating what was happening and when I looked up in the sky I saw many flags hanging in the sky. These were flags of different countries but one of them was peculiar, it had the name JESUS on it written in bold hanging in the air. This was a remarkable dream to me and the most thing that drew my attention was the 40 men who escorted me to the Yacht, all dressed up in white and singing 'Illohi!, Illohi!'. Again, what were those flags all about?!

CHAPTER 14

KEEPING IT ALL SECRET

As soon as I got baptised I became a Christian, a follower of Jesus Christ, which meant that I renounced my Islamic faith to accept the Christian faith; but the fact of the matter was that I wasn't feeling comfortable to disclose my secret to anyone yet. I was worried about a lot of things and especially hurting my mother's feelings. So I lived with this for a long time without telling anyone, the only people who knew about this were my young daughters. They knew that they should not talk to anyone about our conversion and I made them aware of the consequences sometimes people face when they convert from Islam to Christianity, but from where I came from unless I was the first one to convert I've never heard of anyone executed because of converting to Christianity, we have lived along side the Christians peacefully from as far as I could remember, we even went to school together. My main fear was to do with my own family, from my own mother down to my own sons who were now grown up young men – one even with his own family. I just couldn't face them and tell them the truth because from my own understanding of Islam, I knew how this would affect them, my mother would really be disappointed. It would be like I had put them to shame, they would have no place to hide their faces, yes my mother, but especially my brother, a famous man in Zanzibar by his profession but also zealous in his faith. He is also well known in the Zanzibar community living in the UK. Rumours would also spread to the Middle East as people of Zanzibar have close ties in Oman and the Emirates where my sons live. So looking at the whole thing the whole world would be talking about me and the shame would affect the whole family including the relatives, so I was thinking how I could do this.

Getting back to my own home now, you can imagine how life would be being a secret convert living with a Muslim husband, how could I practice my faith in the same place. My husband did not know about it so how could I practice my faith in peace while I tried my best to keep it all secret. Praying was the main thing that worried me in the house because as a Christian you do not pray like a Muslim, and even though my husband was a moderate Muslim he would always keep to his daily prayers so he would wonder if he didn't see me praying. My best bets were the afternoon prayers, for those days that I would be off work and he would be always at work, which was some kind of a relief but at times when we were all at home it was extremely difficult to pray. So if the husband would be in the room and I wanted to pray I had to portray myself as a Muslim praying in Islamic way while in fact I would be reciting the Lord's prayer, giving thanks and directing my prayers to God as I needed. Things were even worse in the morning and night prayers because my husband would always be resting in the bedroom and as it is said 'eyes have no curtains,' so of course he would be watching. He would be even more suspicious if I changed rooms every day.

As a mother I also had to teach my children about the new faith as much as I could and during these difficult times it was mainly to understand the basics, so I taught them how to pray, how to reason and be bold in prayer, thanksgiving, reading the Bible, reciting especially the Lord's Prayer, and to understand the differences in the Christian faith such as between the Christian Churches. At these times it was difficult for me to even sit with my children and read the Bible with them but they would try by themselves from time to time. In fact, even keeping the Bible in the house was another issue because this was not an Islamic Book so I had to hide it carefully in a place that no one else could go or see except myself and the children. The only Bible I had at that time was the one that the Lord had sent me through Rod, it was my treasure so I wouldn't always feel safe sharing it with the children. Eventually they managed to get two more Bibles for themselves from the Church which made me more worried fearing that they may not handle them properly; and in fact I was right, because sometime later one of the Bibles disappeared from the secured place my daughter had kept in her bedroom. She told me it disappeared when her older brother came home for a visit from Oman, he was using her bedroom for that time. So only God knew where the Bible went but I didn't feel comfortable about it at all!

Fasting was not so hard to keep secret because in Islam it usually happens once a year even though people can fast as they wish in a year. In fact it had taken me along time to come out of Islamic way of fasting because I was rooted in this. My mother taught me to fast when I was 10 years old so it took me many years to come out of the habit; it was like a way of life to me. I don't miss it much because as Christians we still fast but not in a prescribed way as it is in Islam. Christians fast in a different way and fasting is usually appointed by the Holy Spirit who will pass the message either through the Pastors or Ministers of the Church or to the individuals themselves depending upon their prayer. In Christianity fasting is considered as part of a specific prayer for a specific reason or purpose and can take place at any time during the year; the length and intensity of it varies upon the purpose and the decision made. So with this one I was more comfortable because I could fast at any time; and when it comes to Ramadhan, the prescribed month for fasting in Islam I went ahead with it as a cover for many years. But the Lord is good, when He saw me behaving this way, He would sometimes talk to me expressing His views about my behaviour, it frustrated Him. It was a long journey but I finally managed to change my behaviour and stay out of it.

Another thing was going to Church, this was more than a nightmare! Because I didn't know what to tell my husband when I wanted to go, after all, he was my husband, so off course he would want to know my whereabouts. There were times when Rod would call me and ask if I would go to Church but I would always say no, I couldn't, it was so difficult. I actually regret one time when he told me to go to Church because there was something that the Lord wanted to do for me; and I said I couldn't go, most of the time it was so hard. In my trials however, I tried to sneak out a few times and went to worship at Churches, I once went with Rod in his area and a couple of times I went to my local Churches in my area. One time I went to that tiny little Church where I ended up upset, I also went to worship at New Wine Church one time but I wasn't at rest at all because I didn't feel free to worship, and even though no one might notice me I would always be full of fear and really shake when I come out of the Church. I just had this feeling in my head that I was being watched so after this occasion at New Wine Church I never went to Church anymore for fear of being caught.

I continued to keep things this way for seven years until I felt suffocated and could not keep it anymore, so one day I thought enough is enough and broke the news.

CHAPTER 15

CONFESSION TO MY FAMILY

Time went by and my spirit yearned to speak to family about my conversion, it was too hard for me to hold it in any more. My heart started burning, I felt guilty for the length of time I had taken keeping things to myself without telling my family the truth, by now it was almost seven years since my baptism. So I made up my mind to break up the ice one way or the other, and on the 2nd August 2009, I knew it was time. I started it by first talking about the Gospel to one of my relatives living in Leicester; this is one of my relatives rooted in Islam, a very difficult person to converse with about the Gospel, which is also known as 'Injeel' in Islam. In fact, as he grew in his Islamic faith he would put his utmost effort in it, not only in his family to keep up Islamic ways but also participating in congregations to do with Islam and supporting his relatives in Islamic rituals. He had much interest in debates about Jesus Christ and what he thought is based on his understanding of the Gospel in line with Islam.

In my conversation with him that day he seemed polite on the phone and although he was always approachable in character I did not expect him to react that way. So I was really happy to at least be able to talk to him and advise him to read the Bible without fear. I also felt free to argue with him a little bit about Christianity. Just to be able to initiate my thoughts with him about Christianity was a great moment to me, I thought I had done a great job, and took courage to overcome my fear. My perception were just right, my cousin did what I anticipated he would do after our little discussion, he informed my other cousin in London whose relationship with my brother is even closer. From this moment forward, rumours started to spread about me all over the country, even in Africa and Arabia where our relatives are; but I was yet to hear from my own brother.

The next thing that came to my mind was to talk to my ex-husband about this so I made arrangements to meet with him. It was on the 31st August 2009 when I called him, just about a month after my divorce; he agreed to meet with me the next day. I started the talks with the divorce issues and despite everything else I still wanted to save my marriage so I told him I still believed he was my husband. He did not agree with that, instead he asked me for forgiveness and wished he was left alone to start his new life. He said he had now gone too far in his life and wasn't looking forward to go back. He said he knew his child would be alright and would be well looked after, it was obvious that he had no more interest in the marriage and was prepared for whatever had to come. I had no chance about that, it was obviously over, but I didn't want him to think that that was the only thing I wanted to discuss with him, so at that point, I took courage and told him about my new faith in Jesus Christ which was the main reason of my request to see him.

It wasn't easy to begin with but my strength was in God, I prayed for it before hand that day before I went to meet him; so I said to him 'I believe that Jesus Christ is God, He is that one God that we all believe in.' I told him I had been investigating many things that God had been showing me for the last 6 years and had now come to the point that the things I saw could only be done by God Himself and no one else, which makes me believe that Jesus is God. In fact, I expected him to be shocked and angry but he seemed confused and never said much, except, 'Whoever has been telling you about these things? And in which book does it say that He is God?' I said to him it is the things that He is showing me, no one else can do except God, and it is written in the 'Injeel' (Gospel) that He is God.

I was surprised that he did not argue with me but instead he insisted that I should never take his daughter to Church and that he had never heard these things before in his life. He then said to me if I believe in what I have told him then I should go to Church, there is no point in fasting. He mentioned fasting because it was the month of Ramadhan in Islam so he thought I was fasting; he said these things in frustration. I remained calm and continued talking, I said to him there is fasting in Christianity but not necessarily in Ramadhan as people mainly do in Islam. I also promised him that I will not take his daughter to Church, though in my heart I knew that wouldn't be the case, I trusted my Lord in that knowing that He will do what is needed to save my child, and even him, her father, amen. After all, the Lord had already told me all the way back that 'My family will be saved' so I had no doubt about that. I made sure that this one would not hear the news from other people, he would know the truth from my own lips.

A few weeks later after my first attempt with my cousin, I started receiving phone calls, even from overseas, asking me about my conversion, they all had doubts about it, they weren't sure. One particular person, who even though he is a relative had never had much interest in my family or my affairs, who I could not remember the last time he had spoken to me, phoned me and asked me if what he had heard was true. I told him you've heard it correctly, yes I have changed my faith. He said he just wanted to hear it from my own mouth so he ended the conversation.

The rumours were now out of hand so I expected to hear anything at any time from my brother or the head of our family (Ali, our first cousin on my father's side, who has known us since we were born and took the responsibility of our marriage affairs and care in the absence of my father who died when we were very young.) This man is like a father to us. However, I intended to inform my family abroad when I went there on holiday. I expected to be there in December 2010, so I would sit down with especially my mother and told her the whole story myself, I wanted to do it myself in front of her. However, as rumours continued, my cousin Ali became suspicious and sent me a text message demanding the truth from what he was hearing from here in the UK and in Zanzibar. He told me that he had heard about my conversion to Christianity from my brother, who in turn had heard the news from my cousin in London, so he requested that I called him as soon as I could (as it was very expensive for him to call me from overseas).

As soon as I received his text I informed my family and I could see that my daughters were worried a lot about it but I told them it was time that my people knew, so let it be. I prayed to my Lord for fear of not knowing their responses but I trusted Him in everything. As I expected, the news had spread as soon as I broke the ice here in the UK, my plan to tell my mother and the rest of my family and relatives abroad was now due, so on the 3rd September 2010, I picked up the phone and made a call to my cousin Ali. He came straight to the point and wanted to know if it was true. He had always been a disciplinary character as far as I could remember but he seemed to be easing up as he advanced in age. I must admit that he went through tough times in his life standing up for the affairs of the entire family and not just our family, especially in the controversial situations like marriages. Now in this situation I knew that I had to be careful in my approach so at first I asked him from where did he hear these news; he stumbled a little bit but told me it was from my own brother as soon as he heard it from my cousins in the UK, therefore he wanted to make sure if it was true by hearing it from my own voice.

That day I confessed to him that I changed my faith and briefed him about the whole thing since it started. Confessing to him was confessing to the whole family as I knew he would inform everybody else in the family but I seriously warned him about my mother, I told him I wanted to do it myself when I get there. He agreed with me. Then I released everything that was stuck in my heart to him, I did not hide anything anymore. I even told him I had kept this to myself for 7 years but when I thought the time was up I decided to let go in the way I felt comfortable. I told him I had always meant to talk to them when I went home on holiday but unfortunately, it turned out be that he approached me first. Strangely enough, he did not yell at me or rebel against me at all but accepted it with a comment as to why I had kept this from them for a long time, and as human beings we believe that there is life and death; especially when it comes to 'funeral arrangements'. I understood him but I also knew that I wasn't ready to talk to them at that time so I gave my reasons to him. He accepted what I said and we agreed to speak again on the phone but in more detail when I went home on holiday as I expected to visit my family in December. From this point onward, my whole family in Zanzibar and Arabia came to know about me except the information was withheld from my mother as I demanded this because of her ill health. She suffered high blood pressure and angina so I wanted to take it easy with her. It was thought that the news could cause her a sudden death.

On the 4th September 2010, a day after my confession to my family, the Lord spoke to me in my heart saying, 'Psalm 18'. I repeated the words silently in my heart and meant to read the Chapter before I went to bed that night but I then totally forgot and was going to bed instead; so I switched off the lights and kissed my little girl good night and laid down on my bed. But as soon as my head touched on the pillow I heard the voice in my heart again saying, 'Psalm 18'. So I got up and put the lights on and started to read the Chapter. I discovered that it was all about God's protection to me, and it came just after the day I confessed to my family. Hallelujah! How wonderful is our God, I really love Him. Then I understood that the Lord was reassuring me from what He had told me long ago that He will protect me.

On my second phone call home, my cousin told me that my sister fainted when she heard the news and he wasn't sure how long it was going to take before my mother found out about it!

CHAPTER 16

A PRAYER TO MUSLIM FRIENDS

On the 10th July 2010, I received a call for a prayer from my Muslim friend of Pakistani origin, this was a family man with a wife and children living in East London. I knew this man as a kind of a colleague who got on well with me in his occasional visits to share his computer expertise at College. Knowing that I wasn't a Muslim even though my name sounded like one, I wondered why he called me for a prayer but I didn't ignore his call, without hesitation I made arrangements to visit his family the same month.

Though this was my first experience in praying for people, let alone to Muslims, I was so excited about it, but before I went I asked him for the reason for the prayer. He gave me a bit of his background and told me how they struggled in life as a family in the UK. He came into the country as a student long ago and was legally allowed to bring his family with him but as life went on it wasn't easy for him, he felt like he had failed his family, especially when he lost his job when the College he worked for was closed. He believed that things were not just difficult when they came to London but were cursed from home as anything he would touch to succeed in life would end up in failure. He said he saw people he trained himself succeed in life while he always struggled. He didn't see light in life, he wanted to see the end of this curse and God to make a way in their lives.

Knowing that they were Muslims, I didn't tempt them to come to Church for the prayer, I didn't want to lose it, so we agreed on the day and went there with my little girl. They welcomed us well at their home and despite that I had never met his family before, his wife was very welcoming and looking forward to the prayer. Their three children were playing around with my little girl. I aimed the prayer according to their request I didn't involve anything they hadn't asked for, so it was nothing to do with knowing Jesus or an attempt to convert them from their Islamic faith. So after a little introduction about ourselves, I reminded them that I was Christian and would be directing the prayer to Jesus Christ. They said a prayer is a prayer and God is God, so I gave thanks to God and started to pray.

I remembered how people prayed for me at Church and how Rod had prayed for me, so I took courage and stood up in front of them and placed my hands on theirs and started to pray, and despite this being my first experience I did not stumble but needed some adjustment; but as I moved on in prayer I became steady and suddenly spoke in confidence about a lot of things and as words flowed out of my mouth I became a bit suspicious of myself, so I paused once just to listen to myself and find out if what I was actually saying was coming from me or it was something else. I also felt a very close presence of God during the prayer. As I went ahead praying the couple became so emotional and tears dropped in lines from their eyes. At the end of the prayer, they opened their eyes and said they never had a prayer like that before, it was a good prayer. I stayed with them for a little while and then went home.

Approximately two weeks after the prayer I received another phone call from my friend asking me for another prayer but he also wanted me to hear the important news from his wife after the first prayer. I confirmed that I would visit them again soon, so on 24/07/2010 I went back to their place and my friend said they needed me to pray for them again but first I should hear some news from his wife, she had something to tell me. She said about two days after the first prayer, she had seen the Lord standing on the air as if flying; she said His head was like light and His features were of a man like the one in the 'Passion of Christ' film. Muslims know Jesus by the name of Issa in the way of Islam; so she said she had seen Issa and praised Him in Islamic way in front of me. Her husband believed that his wife had seen Jesus or (Issa) so he wanted me to hear this; but I asked her how did she know that the Lord looked like the man in the 'Passion of Christ'? They both said that they had never watched these kinds of movies before nor even watched much of the western channels on TV, they would always watch Asian channels, but one day after that prayer they were just browsing through the channels and this movie called 'The Passion of Christ' just popped up in random and they watched it, that was how she came up with that likeness. They said it was a very sad movie. I was so excited to hear the testimony of God and to actually know that He responded to my prayer and revealed Himself to them. I then repeated to her saying, 'So you have actually seen the Lord?' And she said, 'Yes.' I praised the Lord for what He had done and told the couple a little bit more about my own testimony on how I came to know about Jesus Christ. I told them about what had made me convert from Islam to Christianity.

The other thing they said to me was that the situation they had been in was slightly easing up so they wanted a follow up prayer, so I started to pray. At the end of it the man said, 'These are good prayers and they are different, we don't have prayers like these.' I praised the Lord and told them to believe in the prayers and then I went home. Since then we have become family friends instead of colleagues, we visit each other for different occasions like birthdays and celebrations. Later on they told me their serious situation had eased up and the father, the head of the family, managed to sort out the family and they settled better.

As a result of their testimony I noticed that the Lord our God actually works on our prayers and sometimes performs wonders for those we pray for. By this I felt encouraged to pray for people, it felt so good to know that God responded to what I had prayed for by revealing Himself to them. Although these people were complete strangers to me it didn't seem they were to the Lord, He loves everybody, and after all, we all belong to Him except that some of us still don't know Him. This was my first test for prayers for people other than my own family and according to their testimony it has proved to be working. The testimony boosted my confidence and I won't hesitate to try another one. I thank the Lord, I am grateful and honoured that I am one among the many that He has appointed for His own glory and honour. Amen.

CHAPTER 17

MY MOTHER'S DEATH

Was I to blame?
On the 3rd November 2010, I received a phone call from Zanzibar informing me about my mother's death. It was during election times and because of political unrest during those times she was advised to take a holiday to Dar-es-Salaam, the capital of Tanzania, in case of trouble in Zanzibar. So she travelled there with my niece to stay with my cousin and her mother, my mother's favourite sister, who was also there during those times. Unfortunately, my mother who had suffered from angina and high blood pressure for a long time became ill one night and her condition deteriorated around midnight and she suddenly passed away. I was told that she suffered a heart attack while sleeping around midnight and her normal tablets were no help.

It was about 5 o'clock in the morning in London when I heard the news and my mother's body would already have been transported back to Zanzibar by the earliest private flight. To be honest, I didn't even know that she was sent to Dar-es-Salaam for a while but that wouldn't have been a concern to me, she was alright. However, when I heard the phone ringing at 5 o'clock in the morning, I expected the worst, I knew it wouldn't be a normal call, so I picked up the phone and saw my sister in-law's number displayed on the screen. I didn't like it, I straight away thought it could be my mother, and so she broke the news. I was devastated and started screaming from my guts; as you could imagine,

I didn't get the chance to even say good-bye to her let alone tell her my testimony, and according to Islamic customs the funeral has to take place within the 24 hours, so from the moment I heard the news I had to wait until 9 o'clock in the morning for the offices to open before I could book the flight. The worst thing was I didn't even have enough money for my ticket, I had to ask my colleague for a favour.

Waiting for 4 hours that morning was like waiting for 4 days to me. I was the first person at the travel agency that morning but despite the effort it was so hard to get the flight that day and my expectations of catching up with the funeral were very low. I was told that the funeral could be delayed until I arrived for exceptional reasons but I wasn't sure, I thought that because of my situations as a convert they had no good reasons to wait for me.

After I had given up hope of travelling the same day, my cousin, the one who broke the news about me, called me and said he had found a travel agent in East London who might be able to help. So I phoned them and managed to get an early flight for the next day, my cousin said at least you would be there within the first three days of gathering, I thought it was a good advice, so I flew away the next morning and got home late in the afternoon. As I had expected, there was no one in our house as our funerals are handled at my uncle's house in the countryside, but thank God our neighbour was around, she received me with compassion and sympathy. She offered me a shower and some food at her place. Even though I wasn't hungry I touched the food to show my appreciation. However, the food did not go down because of my persistent cries mourning for my mother.

When I was ready to go, she also offered her transport and even accompanied me to the countryside where the gathering was taking place, she was very compassionate to me. As I approached the place, I saw about 200 people gathered among my family and relatives outside my uncle's house reciting the Qur-an and offering prayers for the deceased as is the custom for the first 3 days of the funeral. I wasn't surprised by the number of people because my mother came from a very large family, but she was also very famous and my brother, her son, is very well known in the country as one of the Entrepreneurs in Building Construction. I ran out of strength as I approached the crowd so I couldn't move on my own, I didn't faint though, when they realised it was me two of my cousins came fast and held my hands on each side and walked with me to the lobby, other people in the crowd were all gathering outside the lobby. When I got in I saw my sister sitting with all my aunties, my first cousins and many of our close relatives together. As I got myself together all I did was scream, a cry such as I had never done in my life, calling for my Mum very loudly.

My reactions made the whole congregation in the lobby worse provoking loud cries from everybody. I was seated in the corner beside close members of my mother's family; and as I looked around I saw one of my mother's sisters, who looked like a twin to her, sitting next to me. This aunt always confused people because she looked so like my mother, people always thought they were twins but they were actually not. She was comforting me and of course looking at me, but as she looked at me she wasn't aware that I was seeing the image of my mother which made things worse, so I ended up screaming and screaming. It was like looking at my mother sitting next to me!

All my mother's sisters and remaining brothers were at the gathering, and the one who was with her in Dar-es-Salaam was sitting on the other corner; so after a while I went to say hello to her, so I sat with her for a while as she couldn't move easily because of arthritis. She knew what I wanted to hear, so she told me the whole story about mother's last days when they were together, she told me my mother told her she had always wanted to be with her when she passed away, so she died in her knees. My mother was a leading figure in her family and beloved by all her brothers and sisters, these people managed to keep us their siblings close together so we grew up as a close family. She was the one who knew what happened in those last moments so I felt contented.

Anyway my brother was in charge of the gathering

alongside my sister and one of our first cousins from one of our uncles' daughters. They had to feed a large crowd for three days at the gathering, so at lunch time the next day, my brother, my sister and my cousin went inside the house to discuss about it. A few minutes later, believing that I was part of the family, I got myself up and followed them in the back kitchen even though they didn't call me, but when they saw my face they looked at each other wondering what I was doing there. It was all in their faces they didn't have to explain. Anyway when I heard them talking about the money, I said I had something to give but it wasn't much at the time because I hadn't changed my money into the local currency yet. So I took about 70,000 Shillings I had borrowed from our neighbour in the city just to get me round until I changed my money, which was roughly about eighty pounds in Sterling at the time,and gave it to my brother just to add it into what he had. He didn't seem pleased with that so he said these words openly, 'We can add this as part of the donation we are receiving', and the rest of them, my sister and cousin gave me that daring look. After he had said that, they gave a clear impression that they wanted to be left alone with their business. I did get the message and left them alone and went back to the lobby. I felt demoralised treated that way, like I was not part of them, they treated my money as a donation from a stranger, and the money wasn't ignored because it was a small amount, no, it was because of me. This attitude affected me a lot and remained in my memory for quite a long time, hurting me every time I thought of it, but it was only the beginning of a lot worse to come!

The gathering went on for three days and on the fourth day everybody went their own ways but some of my cousins and my half-sister, who came from the other Island, decided to stay with us in the city for an extra week, to give us moral support and comfort before they went home. We were then visited by our regular relatives especially our close cousins living near the area; and as we discussed about the loss at those times, my cousin, the one who gave me that eye in the kitchen told me that my mother was suspicious and had once asked her if I had changed my faith. I asked her, 'what did you say?' She said she told her she'd never heard about it, but she said it because she didn't want to hurt her feelings, especially because of her ill health. She said my mother was sick so she didn't want to risk it, but deep down she said she knew about it and that was what had killed her! So she blamed me for this and because she did then my feelings were they all felt the same way. My sister was present when she said that but as she is she just kept quiet, and I remembered the warning well when I was told that the situation could kill my mother if she found out about it. As a matter of fact, my mother was first diagnosed with angina and high blood pressure in 1995 and I was the one who took her to hospital in London for diagnosis, she had from it suffered since then. So I asked them, 'was I to blame for her death because I changed my faith?' In many ways this was how many people would see this, whether they were my relatives or not, but I asked them, 'would she not have died if I hadn't changed my faith?' They said, 'she would have died but this could be the cause of it.' In fact it was too much for me to bear.

As soon as we got home to the city, my cousin Ali, the one who spoke to me on the phone in London, came to see me the next day inquiring about our discussion regarding my conversion. He wanted a meeting with me the next day. Because it was too soon for me, being just three days after the loss of my mother, I wasn't really comfortable about it. I felt like they had no remorse about the mourning of my mother, possibly because they were always there with her or could see her anytime, so they were contented. But I thought they should realise that because I wasn't there I would need more time for myself or at least if they could respect my feelings. It was just too soon for me to engage in anything else at that time, let alone the severe headaches I suffered from persistent cries. So I postponed the meeting that day because I wasn't ready and in fact, I didn't feel well either. Ali accepted my apology for that day but pressed on for the re-arrangements as soon as possible. For some reasons my headaches persevered and I started feeling dizzy at times, then I realised I hadn't taken my iron tablets since I had arrived, which could have been the cause for drowsiness because I was anaemic. So the next time he tried I still had to tell him I wasn't well, which he didn't like, he thought I was making it up trying to escape the discussion, so he insisted we meet the next day. I said to him I will come but I wasn't feeling well.

The night before the meeting I confined myself in a room praying to my God to give me strength and to be with me in the meeting and in everything else; I said to my God that I have chosen Him over men and asked for His presence. That day I also texted my Pastor in London to pray for me as I was facing rejection, my Pastor replied to me saying, 'Salma, I will pray for you, but whatever they do, pray to God to forgive them, for they do not know what they do.' I also had one of other Pastors from Church prayed for me when I was on my way to the airport on the day I was leaving London for Zanzibar. I trusted my God in everything but I felt like facing the canon.

The next day arrived and in the afternoon my cousin Ali came to collect me and said we were going to have the meeting at his house. However, after a couple of miles he stopped the car on the way and started talking to me. He said we could no longer go to his house for the meeting and instead we would be meeting at my brother's house. I asked him why a sudden change? He mumbled a bit and then said it was a bit difficult for him to take me to his house. I understood it would be because of the reactions from his family as I understood their frustrations. On the other hand, I also thought it could have been a planned agenda, it might have been they weren't sure I would agree to have the meeting at my brother's house so he decided to test me on the way. As a matter of fact, I couldn't get a straight answer but I didn't want to strain him. In fact, I expected it to be there in the first place. I also felt sorry for him trying his best as a leader of the family but I had already told him in advance that I will respect their call but will not tolerate commands! I knew they worked in a close team structure.

CHAPTER 18

IN THE MEETING ROOM

Round one:
When we arrived at my brother's house I looked up in the sky for a signal from my God, and yes, His signal was there, He came with me. The bright moon glowed in the sky surrounded by many bright stars alongside it and there stood that sparkling star adjacent to it. Nobody else noticed this, they wouldn't understand it anyway. I noticed we entered the house through the back door into a large study room where I was seated. My brother has a wife and children living in the house, but they had never come up to meet with me, even on this day when I was actually sitting in their own house in their back room.

Inside the room, there were many people most of whom were my own close relatives except the Sheikh, the Islamic Priest. I was asked to sit next to my uncle, my father's cousin, in a row that faced the rest of the people in the room. As I looked in front of the room I saw one of my cousin's husband on the left side, this was the husband of one of my cousin's sisters, the one who broke the news about my conversion, I usually got on well with him with jokes. Next to him was my brother, then the Sheikh (the Priest) followed by my first cousin from my father's side. There were two formerly Catholic men who had converted to Islam sitting opposite me. The last man, also a Catholic convert, sat in the corner on the right hand side of the room next to my cousin Ali, the one who brought me to the meeting.

My brother was the head of the meeting, and apart from the Sheikh and the ex-Catholic men everybody else knew each other. Everyone was keen to hear my confession and especially the background reasons behind the conversion. Before I started my testimony I openly told them about my health that I wasn't well that day but I respected their call and came over. I told them I felt a bit dizzy and had not completely recovered from the severe headaches I suffered, however, I was willing to continue with the discussion for at least 2 hours. When hearing this, my brother jumped in and said the 2 hours I was proposing wouldn't be enough, it will depend upon when the discussion will end; especially because he had invited people from the mainland for me specifically for this occasion and it had cost him their return tickets to Dar-es-Salaam. It was in his face that he didn't care much about my health. I felt pressured by his answers. Surely this wasn't my problem as I didn't invite those men neither was I informed of their presence, however, I didn't want to invite an argument nor was I scared, but I told him I would have to be sent home if I wasn't able to continue. I also added that it would be alright with me if they would like to re-arrange the meeting for another discussion while I was still in the country.

After I had given as much as I could remember about my testimony, that was when my brother told me about the three Catholic men who converted to Islam that he had invited to the meeting to help me clear my understanding about Christianity. He then apologised that they had not initially informed me about this, he then asked me if I was alright with that before he brought them in; another insult from him, he was asking about my opinion when he had already got the men there. So when I first entered the room those people weren't actually sitting there yet, they were asked to wait in a different room nearby while I was talking about my testimony.

I honestly did not like to be taken by surprise, they saw this in my face; so before I answered him I looked at my cousin Ali who was by now worried a bit, but then I said, 'It's alright, I'm OK.' At this point my brother went to get them from the other room where they were all waiting and brought them into the back room where the discussion was taking place. As they entered the room my brother looked at me and said, 'Don't be scared.' I wasn't sure whether he was comforting me or promoting fear on me. I knew for sure they had all worked on this together as a team hoping that I might be intimidated by meeting with not one but three born and bred as Catholics who obviously knew more about Christianity then me. On one hand they might be right that these men were born into the faith, studied it and practiced well before me but on the other hand they didn't realise that they didn't have my 'Testimony'.

As a matter of fact I was angry with my brother, not scared at all. I asked myself what was the need for all these tricks! I then recalled a few things which started to add up together, first the change of plan on our way to the meeting, then, the hidden information about the presence of the converted Catholics and the way the meeting started, with initially only members of the family and relatives and then the gentlemen being called in to join the discussion. These men were originally from the main land of Tanzania not from Zanzibar.

Anyway, the men were then called in and introduced to me and were given a summary of what I had testified to the team, then the meeting continued. In my testimony, I tried to explain as much as I could remember about my experiences and revelations I had encountered as I explained earlier in this book. During the meeting, there were certainly many aspects of my testimony I missed out at that time but are now all included in this book.

When hearing my testimony my brother and the rest of my relatives asked me many questions about my conversion to Christianity before the Catholic men were brought in to join the meeting. They wanted to know if I understood my religion (Islam) well and if I did, what had made me change my faith! They continued to ask me if I was persuaded or influenced to change my faith by anybody like a boyfriend or so while they all knew that I was married. Their overwhelming insults continued with another severe question like 'how much money were you paid for this?' In return, I remained calm but reminded them about my background as a practical

Muslim who was born and bred in Islamic way, and was not only taught the Qur-an since I was seven but also learnt much about the faith itself as I grew older. In fact I had once got to the point of planning to learn the procedures for women burials as practiced in Islam just before I came to know the Lord. I also told them as a practiced Muslim it had always been in my interest to recite the Qur-an every year, praying for relatives who've gone before us, which is regarded as the only 'gift' or prayer that can reach and help the dead parents as a result of raising up a good Muslim child. Anyway, as I responded to their insults, I also touched about my good character and respect I have to both myself and others including protecting my modesty. I have always believed I was taught and learnt well as I grew in the faith and lived my life to an acceptable standard according to Islam; however, when it came to my conversion it was between me and my God. At the end of my testimony, I thought I testified my reasons for the conversion but they weren't convinced they were good enough for changing my faith.

At the end of my testimony and a series of questions and answers with them, my brother said to me those three once Catholic men would help me understand what I didn't know and might help expand my knowledge of Christianity and hopefully convince me, according to the Bible, that I was wrong converting from Islam. These Catholic men aimed to reference their talk within the Bible so they asked me about the Bible I was using so that we can synchronise the information. In fact they brought in a couple of Bibles or may be more with them! So I told them I did not come in for a formal debate at that time neither was I aware of their visit, I only understood that the meeting will be between me and my family. It was obvious to them that I only happened to meet them at the meeting. So before the discussion started, I wanted to make sure that these men are familiar with the 'rules' of discussion; so I explained that we had to agree on the manner and behaviour during the discussion and that no one's voice should be raised against the other if we don't agree in certain points. We agreed to base our discussion on the New King

James Bible (NKJV), the nearest from the original Hebrew Bible that I'm reading. I had to confess to them however, that even though I am able to refer my conversation to what is said in the Bible I will not necessarily be able to quote from the actual books or verses from it at that time. Fortunately they agreed on that.

I noticed the sequence of the questions from those men that two of them took turns in questioning and giving answers, while the third one acted as a listener. My brother was a 'controller', making sure the rules were followed in the discussion. So the two men were questioning me me a lot of questions referring to the Bible. Their aim was to make it clear to me that Jesus Christ is not God but a Prophet. He was sent by God like all other Prophets, and following Him, God sent the Prophet Muhammad (the Muslim Prophet). My defence to this was yes, He was a Prophet but at the same time He was God in human flesh, so the discussion was mainly based on these concepts. As for me, I gave my answers based on my testimony which is based on the experiences and revelations that God, in the name of Jesus had shown me, as described in this book.

As the discussion went on, many questions were asked for me to testify that Jesus is that God. The men would then reflect my answers to what the Bible says and would read the contexts aloud, especially those verses of the Bible they would see as contradictory, when sometimes Jesus presents Himself as God and sometimes as the Son, especially quoted from the Gospel of John where I mainly based my answers. This cycle of discussion went on for a long time and in as much as I would explain in the areas that Jesus implies Himself as God the men would refer back to those verses they see contradicting, that Jesus also says He is the Son of God. Then I was once asked by my brother saying, 'Don't you see that there is a lot of confusion in the Bible?' Despite my little knowledge of the content of the Bible at that time, I agreed with them the areas within the Gospels that Jesus identifies Himself as the Son, but also insisted on the other side of His Godhead, trying to make it clear to them that there are also many verses in the Gospels, particularly in the Book of John, that the same Jesus implies Himself as God with authority. How can an ordinary person or even a Prophet declare that they are God with authority? I asked, 'Will they not be betraying their own God?' So out of my memory I gave them some examples of what Jesus said in the Gospel of John:

'I and my Father are one' (John 10:30)
'He who has seen Me, has seen the Father' (John 14:9)
'I am in the Father and the Father is in Me' (John 14:11)

'If you believed in Moses, you would believed Me,
for he wrote about Me'
(John 5:46)
'Before Abraham was, I am' (John 18:58)
'No one takes it (His life) from Me, but I lay it down of
Myself. And I have the power to lay it down and I have
power to take it again' (John 10:18)

Those were as much as I could remember at that time. Then one of the three men (a listener) as I have pointed out above, asked me a question about who actually taught me the Bible. I said to him, 'It is Jesus; He is the One who is teaching me.' The man took it as a joke and did not believe me, so he asked me again saying, 'My sister, please tell me who is actually teaching you?' I said to him again, 'It is Jesus, He is the One who is teaching me.' I assume he did not get the answer he had expected, so he decided to give up and kept quiet but turned his head to the rest of the people and said, 'You people think that this lady does not know what she is talking about and doesn't even know anything about the Bible, but I'm telling you that she knows, and she is learning the Word from the Spirit Filled Bible, King James Version, from the Original Hebrew Bible, which has been used in the American Law called 'Dogma'.' To be honest with you I didn't have any idea about the American law or what 'Dogma' meant, but I was amazed by his response to them. In the end, it was like he turned his back from them and supported me instead!

And so somehow there was a blessing in the end out of my perseverance. I just wish I could have told them more from what I know now, that God says in the Bible, 'He will put His law in our minds and write it in our hearts, no more shall every man teach his neighbour, and every man his brother, saying know the Lord, for they all shall know Him, from the least of us to the greatest of us', Jeremiah 31: 31-34. He also said, we shall all be taught by God. Therefore the Holy Spirit teaches us all things; and He is God Himself working in this personality.

It was turning 2 o'clock in the morning since the meeting began, then the priest asked me if I wanted to change back to my Islamic faith, I said to him no, I'm alright. He asked me once again, Are you sure you don't want to change back to Islam? I said, 'No thank you, I don't want to change back to Islam.' Can you imagine their reactions? At that moment I could read in their faces that they wished I did, and suddenly one of my cousins also named Ali broke down in tears claiming, 'Salma!, please remember your parents.' He was sobbing in that corner. But I remained strong, strengthened by the Lord who was present in that room. I did not change my faith, why? Because I know the truth, and this has made me free! As disappointed as they were, to them there was still hope to receive me, however small, so they asked me if I would discuss this again with them as I had suggested in the beginning should we have to end the discussion sooner because of my health, which they didn't bother considering even when I asked them to end it at some point in the discussion because I felt dizzy. Out of this however, meaning as a result of being kept there, I was pleased to have heard from the ex-Reverend who in the end stood up for me instead; so it turned out to be a blessing to me. On the other hand, I don't blame my relatives that much for being so strict in considering my health that day, as I knew in their minds they were aiming for victory, to save me from what they think is the false faith and therefore according to Islam they were saving me from the hell fire. So I try seeing it from my point of view. What if it was one of them who was chosen to receive this Testimony instead of me? How would I have reacted on them as a strong believer? Unfortunately what they missed is the strong revelations I have concluding that Jesus is the Lord, our God and Saviour, the only One who can save our souls from the hell fire; which is so hard for them to understand or shall I say accept? So I said to them I don't mind having a second discussion with them before I leave the country, we just need to arrange for it in good time. Therefore we agreed to have another discussion before I returned to England. At this point my brother asked the priest if I was eligible for my mother's inheritance, the Sheikh (Priest) said no, she is cut out of it because she is no longer a Muslim. So I was cut out from inheriting from my mother because I have become a Christian. My brother didn't look back and tell me anything because I heard it all, it was spoken openly. We ended the discussion at 2 o'clock in the morning, my cousin Ali took me back home. I went straight to bed.

CHAPTER 19

IN THE MEETING ROOM

Round two:
A few days later, my cousin Ali called me on the phone to ask if my headaches had eased and to see if I was still interested and ready for the second discussion. I said I was still interested and would love to meet those men again but I needed some time to sort out my other things as the date for my return to England was near. So we agreed to meet a few days before my departure.

The day came and again my cousin Ali came to collect me from home. As usual I prayed before I went and even texted my close people at Church to pray for me concerning this discussion. This time the meeting did not start late as the first one had. In the meeting room were more or less the same people except that my uncle (my father's cousin) did not come this time nor two of the Catholic converts who were there in the first round. This time my brother chose a different set of the Catholic men, excluding the one who stood up for me and the younger one of the other two. I'm not sure if these men were intentionally excluded or decided themselves to go, however, in their replacement, he chose two different ones to add up with the one who was previously there, therefore he would still have three of these men in place to take up the discussion with me. Again, of these men one was once a 'Reverend' in the Catholic Church in Dar-es-Salaam, the capital of Tanzania in the main land, who is also academically well educated.

My brother opened the discussion by introducing us and giving a brief outline of my conversion, just to give an insight to those other Catholic converts who weren't there in the first round so they would understand my situation. I assume that this may not have been the first time they would have been informed about me but it had to be done in front of me for the benefit of the discussion. I was OK with that anyway. This time the 'Reverend' sat next to me, I was in the same seat as before. The other ones sat opposite me in the corner on the other side of the room; then the discussion started.

The questions went on; I noticed that the 'Reverend' was also the observer, or more or less the same and again I based my answers on my testimony, according to the revelations and wonders I had seen and heard as the Lord had spoken. I also referenced my answers to the Bible, in the bits that I could do at that time, as I did in the previous discussion. Basically they asked me, 'where exactly does it say in the Bible that Jesus is God?', which is one of the main questions many Muslims would ask anyone conveying the message of God from the perspective of the New Testament. One person I know who, was not in that group that day, once said to me if I show him where this is said in the Bible he would convert to Christianity straight away. So when they asked this question again in this round, they basically wanted to bring up the same discussion again in the hope that this time I would get the message; hence, to my assumption, the 'Reverend' was sent in.

As I was prepared to answer, I wanted to get some verses from Bible which would convince them Jesus is God, so I asked for a pardon to use my phone. They agreed, and as they waited I sent a text to two of my Church people in London who I had asked to pray for me while on my way to the first meeting in the first round. I asked them to send me some Bible references in the hope of answering this question. These were my friend Lucy, one of the Ministers and one of other Pastors from our Church. These people, especially my friend Lucy were aware of the situation I was in, surrounded by the kind of judges if you like facing those questions alone far away from England; so they texted back as soon as possible with many possible answers from the Bible, especially from the Gospel of John. They both quoted mainly from John 1:1 to John 1:14 and also some other relevant references. As the texts did not take long to receive, the waiting time was rarely noticed so it didn't seem to bother the group. I assume they didn't even know I was asking for the confirmation or backup from my Church. I suddenly read the references loud to them and asked them to look from these verses in the Bible. All of them were keen on these verses and one at a time interpreted them contextually, pressing in the places where Jesus is conveyed as the 'Son of God', and sometimes the 'Son of Man'. For some reasons, they did not have much interest in John 1:1, it was skipped out most of the time. When I noticed that it was being skipped out, I stressed that we should not ignore the areas that Jesus also implies that He is God, based on those Scriptures. I also stressed the miracles and wonders I had experienced, which I believe could not be performed by man or even Satan, despite his powers. While reviewing the Scriptures, they disagreed with what I said to them, pressing that I mis-understood the Scriptures; they said that the Scriptures do not say that Jesus is God and definitely He is not the Son of God, as according to Islam, God has no Son. As the verses were interpreted, one of the two converts started on the issue about God sending the Helper who will guide people to His faith after Jesus, which provoked my little understanding about the Holy Spirit at that time. This man was one of the Catholic converts, who interpreted the Holy Spirit as referring to Muhammad, the prophet of Islam. He said that God said He will send the Helper, the Spirit of truth to line up people in His faith; and this Helper who is the Spirit of truth, is Muhammad, the Islamic Prophet sent by God after Jesus who is known as Issa in Islam. He continued saying to me, 'So you see, Muhammad is even mentioned in the Bible from a long time ago.' I looked at the man on the eye and said to him that Muhammad is not the 'Helper' that is mentioned in the Bible, nor is he the Spirit of truth that is explained in the Bible. As I had much interest in the concept of the Holy Spirit myself whilst searching for the truth, I could remember

121

this chapter from the Bible very well, even though I could not recall the exact references at the time. So I tried to explain to them who the 'Helper' actually is even though I didn't have my notes with me and they listened attentively. I based my explanations on my general understanding and this is what I said about the 'Helper':

> In the Bible, Jesus said, 'I will send you the Helper, the Spirit of Truth whom the world cannot receive, because it neither sees Him nor knows Him, but you know Him for He dwells with you and will be in you.'
> I also added that Jesus said, 'I will not leave you orphans, I will come to you.'

I tried to expand the meaning of what Jesus said, that after He had gone back to Heaven, He will not leave us orphans but He will come back to us as the 'Holy Spirit'. Then the men searched the Scriptures which they knew very well and read out loud from John 14:16 onwards which were the actual words concerning the Holy Spirit, but they did not believe. I note what Jesus also said in John 14:25-26:

'These things I have spoken to you while being present with you, but the 'Helper', the 'Holy Spirit' whom the Father will send in 'My name' will teach you all things and bring to your remembrance all things that I said to you.'

Based on these Scriptures Jesus said the Holy Spirit will be sent in His name and He will dwell with us forever, therefore I told them it could not have been 'Muhammad' because he didn't live forever, Jesus clearly said in the Scriptures that the Holy Spirit will be sent in His name and will live in us, Jesus also said He will come to us. I then concluded that this is the Holy Spirit that is talked about in the Bible. The Holy Spirit that lives in and dwells with people who believe in Jesus Christ; they know Him and hear His voice. I then related this bit to what Jesus said about His sheep in the Book of John:

> 'I am the good Shepherd and I know My sheep, and **Am known** by My own' (John 10:14),

Also,

'My sheep **hear My voice**, and I know them,
and they follow Me' (John 10:27).

Then I asked them a question, 'if Jesus was only a Prophet, a human being like us, how could He be able to send the Holy Spirit?' They looked at each other and ignored the question. Then one of the converts diverted the issue to the Angel Gabriel as the Holy Spirit, this one is known as 'Jibreel' in Islam, who appeared to Mary or 'Mariam' in Islam and told her about her pregnancy for 'Jesus Christ' but said that the Christians confuse it.

As we continued in the discussion, John 1:1 was burning in me so I stressed it. I asked them why they were skipping this one out. I really wanted them to see the backbone of this Scripture! This time they didn't ignore it, they went back to the Chapter and as they discussed about it, they found something I assume they would already know about, that this same Jesus was the 'Word' that was then made into 'Flesh' and this 'Flesh' then came to live with us, (John 1:14). The two convert 'debaters' were obviously struggling with it and so I confirmed to them saying, 'So the 'Word' was made 'Flesh' and this 'Flesh' came to live with us, and this 'Flesh' is Jesus.' They just looked at me and this was the point of intercession for the 'Reverend' to rescue the group. He joined in at this point and said to them, 'I knew she would get you on this one! John 1:1 is hard to explain.' I locked my conversation here in the hope that they would agree, but to no avail! Instead, they asked me if I wanted to revert back to my faith, Islam. I said no, I do not wish to do that. They did not seem happy but were not aggressive. Then the 'Reverend' said to them, 'She had already made up her mind when she came here, she is an educated woman as well.' This time the meeting ended around mid-night, it wasn't too bad.

As we prepared to go home, the men in their sad faces suggested they offered me some books relating to Christianity to take home for reading. The former 'Reverend' in a Catholic

Church promised to find me a Bible which could clearly prove that the current text is corrupted, he hoped to find this Book at the University of Dar-es-Salaam though had doubts that he would be able to find one, but said he would try his best. He also promised to find me some other literature such as those discussing about the Saints in the Catholic Church and how they became Saints and some other books in Christianity that will give me more insight about the 'Religion' as they call it. They also offered me some books about Islam, as in their heads I did not understand it at all! My brother promised to post these books to me by DHL, the fastest international delivery service, once I arrived in the UK. I appreciated their time and effort and said thank you. Some people exchanged their mobile numbers with me so we could keep in touch. My interest was also in the Sheikh who was the silent member of them all, he said he had interest in hearing more about 'this Book', meaning the Bible, as a result of our little conversation on a particular story about a certain Prophet also called 'Nabii' in Islam, that he found out I also knew about it from the Bible. He was amazed and said, 'I would like to know more about this Book, the Bible, it's interesting!'

When we came out of the house, I looked up for my signals, and there they were! Above the roof of my brother's house the moon glowed brightly in the middle of the night with that sparkling star close to it.

The next morning I saw my sister's face so sad as the situation did not turn out as she had expected. So while in the living room, I said to them all, let's wait and see the glory of God, one day we will see where He is taking us. My two best friends invited me to their homes, one for dinner and the other for the evening tea, before I left the country; and while I was in my friend's house, the wife of my youngest daughter's uncle, took me out for a walk in the nearest local park by the sea and said to me, 'I tried to tell them not to set you up in the group but they didn't listen, I knew it wouldn't work.' I had to ask her what she meant about that and she said while this whole thing was being arranged, she had a telephone conversation with my best friend and a onetime colleague of mine in Zanzibar that they should not set me up in a group session because I am a teacher, as they would simply create the environment for me. She said, 'We said to them they should have it done in one to one.' To be honest I found this really amusing and we both laughed out loud! Then we walked home and had that lovely special dinner before I was taken to my other best friend for the evening tea. The day was so exciting that when I left the first house I had forgotten my niece who had come with me, she got carried away chatting with my friend's girls! So she had to be sent to my friend's house after I had arrived at the place. I enjoyed the evening tea with my friend and her family, then she drove me home still trying to convince me to return to Islam. She gave me an example of her own niece who had converted to the Catholic faith in America. She said to me her niece returned to Islam after she was convinced that she was wrong, and Islam is the righteous faith. I said to her not all Christians are Catholics and there are different dimensions in Christianity but I have a strong testimony that God has testified to me to make me believe that 'Christianity', which is the faith involving the teaching of Jesus Christ comes from God and Christians are the followers of Christ, who is God. She was polite as in her nature, she didn't interfere with me, she dropped me home and we wished each other the best, we said we will see each other again next time and she went home.

The time came and I was ready to leave the country and come back home in England. My other Son, at the time living in Zanzibar, and my sister's children came to the airport with me. Surprisingly, my brother also turned up just before the check in time to be with me; and when the time was up we said our goodbyes then I checked in and waited for my flight. But suddenly, out of the blue, I saw someone coming towards me walking through the restricted area where no one would be allowed to enter except the passengers waiting for their flights; and there she was, my best friend, the one who is married to my husband's brother carrying something in a carrier bag. It was amazing to see her there, she said it was emergency at the controls so she was allowed a few minutes to see me, only to find out she brought me some of her books about Islam! She said, 'Promise me you will read them, they will help you a lot.' I said I did not have a hand luggage with me and didn't really like to carry anything heavy in my handbag but she begged me to take them with me so I appreciated her effort, I didn't want to disappoint her. I don't think she knew I would have a parcel of them when I got home.

I arrived home after ten days abroad and although difficult I tried to resume my life as normal, but it was more or less impossible at first. I would still have sudden tears coming from out of the blue when I remembered my mother. My daughters have been very supportive to me comforting me in those difficult times. We have all been in this together, I know that the Lord is my strength and my comfort and has always been there for me. When it came to the extreme times and I would just break down in tears, I would hear myself praying in tongues from inside me which gave me comfort and healing, when it happened I would naturally calm down and move on with life and as life goes on I continue working and looking after my family, even though tribulations did not seem to cease easily.

CHAPTER 20

REJECTION FROM MEMBERS OF FAMILY

On my return to England, I realised that most members of my family and relatives deserted me as a result of not reverting back to Islam. Although I had actually tried to find time to read all the books given to me by my friend and those sent to me as promised, none of them convinced me otherwise, I found no weight in them as I read through them, I could not compare them to what I now know. I must admit however, I was very much interested in understanding the history of the Saints from the books that were sent to me as I had never read about them before, so in this instance I was pleased by them, because it is discussed in detail about what the Saints did in their lives in order to become Saints; in the contrary, this knowledge had only drawn me closer and closer to my Lord and Saviour as I read their stories as Jesus said, He is *the way, the truth* and *the life*,' and that no one comes to the Father except through Him. John 14:6.

Also in some of the books I have been sent, it is noted that Muhammad (the Prophet of Islam) is also mentioned in the Bible even by Moses in the Book of Deuteronomy when he said the Lord will raise up a Prophet like him from among their brothers and He will put His words in His mouth and He shall speak to them all that the Lord has commanded Him, Deuteronomy 18:18. Based on this verse it is believed in Islam that the 'One' appointed to come is Muhammad. However, if we take a step back in Deuteronomy 18:15, Moses wrote, 'The Lord your God will raise up for you a Prophet like me 'from your midst', 'from your brothers', Him you shall hear.' Therefore referring back to this Scripture we can find that when the Lord was speaking to Moses in the desert about the 'One to come', Moses was engaged in the midst of the congregation with the children of 'Israel' his brothers, and was telling them that the 'One to come' will be chosen from 'amongst themselves' in the latter times; therefore, the 'One to come' would be from among the children of Israel who used to be called 'Jacob'. In this Chapter, God also states that the Prophet He would raise shall speak in 'His name', and following this then comes Deuteronomy 18:18 as explained above. This prophecy of Moses is found to be fulfilled by Jesus Christ, the 'One from their midst', from the line of Judah when He came on earth in flesh. The same prophecy is also emphasised by Peter in the Book of Acts, 3:22-23 elaborating the 'One to come'; and in John 5:43, Jesus confirms to the children of Israel that He has come in His Father's name even though many did not believe Him, He said, 'I have come in My Father's name and you do not receive Me', which connect back to that Prophet in Deuteronomy 18:15 who shall speak in 'His name' that is, God's name. In John 6:63, Jesus goes on to say that 'It is the Spirit who gives life, the flesh profits nothing, the words I speak to you are Spirit and are life'. So how do we interpret this then when He says His words are Spirit and are life, and, it is the Spirit who gives life! This raises the question as to who Jesus is. I do not wish to get out of context here but this Person, Jesus, also tells us in John 10:18 that no one can take His life away from Him but He laid it down by Himself; He has power to lay it down, and has power to take it again, which makes it clear that no ordinary human being can practice this.

In one of the books I was sent, I also noticed some miracles which are said to be envisioned or practised by Prophet Muhammad, such as when he had a vision or dream of the depth of the earth and what lies underneath it when no one else had known about it, etc. It could be argued however that visions like these are recorded in the Book of Jonah and others in the Bible. Getting back to the point, my thoughts, despite reading all these books, remained the same and even became stronger as I also know what has been revealed to me by the Lord Jesus Christ Himself. Therefore by the great works of God that even God had to do to kindly convince me He is the One, I can only thank Him for His mercy.

As my family did not get much response from me since my return, they must have talked about the situation between themselves to see if I had reached any decisions of turning back to Islam, because two months after my return, my cousin, the one who broke the news of my conversion to my family, started to check on me through the phone, asking how I was doing. Remember this is two months later after I had arrived home and before that it was all quiet, to me it was obvious that he had no interest in my well-being except to find out where I stood on my decision to remain a Christian. His phone calls then became a weekly routine until I plainly said to him I had made up my mind and will never change back to Islam. This is when he said, 'I wash my hands out of this now', and since then he has never phoned me back or checked on me until this day as I complete this book. So again, the interest was in Islam, not my affairs or well-being.

As I didn't agree with their decision, I was doomed to be cut off from my some members of my family and relatives, including any participation in ceremonies or gatherings, I was left alone; but my children despite their bitterness in this, they didn't abandon me. My sister and my cousin Ali did not desert me, they took the bitterness and kept hoping for the best, also a few cousins from home could at least speak to me even though I knew they were hurt inside. Since then there have been no phone calls, let alone visits, from any of my relatives here in England or abroad except my communication with my cousin Ali and my sister. Mr Ali says, 'I can't abandon you, you are my sister'. Just a side note, there is not much of a difference between a first cousin and a sister in our culture, we are regarded as close as brothers and sisters, therefore it is not strange for my cousin Ali to call me a sister. I do still receive occasional calls and sometimes texts from him, he is not willing to lose hope about me.

When my other cousin in Leicester found out that I wasn't going back to Islam and my decision was final, he actually phoned me to say that they do not get along with people like that, meaning the ex-Muslims, which basically meant I should forget about them. This one is married to my niece, a daughter of my first cousin on my father's side, he is my second cousin from my mother's side. Can you imagine that my own niece wouldn't speak to me? In fact, I am abandoned by almost all my relatives here in England, no one wants to know about me because of my conversion. Strangely enough, only my ex-husband would sometimes call to speak to his child.

Because of my conversion, I have never even received condolences for the loss of my mother from any my relatives here. One of them bumped into me in the City Centre, so she said she was sorry, the other one even refused to speak to me while we were still in the gathering at home. It was too much to find out that she was actually asked if she wanted to speak to me when she phoned in that day but she refused to do so; and it wasn't difficult for me to understand what she said on that phone call because I was sitting next to the person she was talking to in the room. Also the facial expressions of other people sitting near me were apparent, they were filled with disappointments as they looked at me; and though I didn't feel good at it I just had to face it. In fact, my immediate family, my daughters and I are excluded from it all, no weddings, no gatherings, not even funerals, let alone visits; but the one thing I must always remember is that my two sons and their families who live far away from me in Arabia have never neglected me nor cut me off as their mother even though in reality I know they are hurting. My conversion to Christianity has disappointed them and humiliated them in front of their relatives and friends, but the worst thing is that because of the partition in faith, we cannot serve one another if one of us passes away according to Islam, it also interferes with inheritance. This makes it too much to bear but I have a promise and I intend to wait for it for as long as it takes. I know Jesus never fails, He does not go back on His word and His word does not come back to

Him empty. I trust Him. He told me all my family will be saved. Amen.

Trying to understand my people's reactions, I could see why they are angry about me – which does not necessarily mean they don't like me. In their view, I have committed a sin which will take me to hell fire and they are trying to do their best to save me and the children from it. I can also understand the actions my brother took trying to help me come out of the situation, despite of his peculiar approaches, such as arranging for prayers throughout Zanzibar for me and also liaising with my cousins here in England for prayers in the mosques throughout London so that many people would pray for me and the children in the hope that I return to Islam. So there is no doubt he is concerned about me. Also the meetings he had arranged gathering people of Christian origin to try to help me come to an understanding of what I was doing, which involved effort and costs on his part, therefore even though he didn't consult me he did it for me.

Anyway, in the second meeting it was said that I was put under 'witchcraft' by whoever made me convert to Christianity, as it had proved so difficult for them to revert me back to Islam. When all their effort had come to no avail, it is understandable that they are angry with me but believe me I love them all. I love my brother and wouldn't blame him for his reactions, neither do I blame anyone else about this, instead I praise the Lord and wait, thinking what would I have done if the Lord had chosen somebody else from my family to break the news of Jesus instead of me. Thinking of how I was as a Muslim I could have been worse than them. Saying this however, does not mean I don't get emotional, oh yes, I do; but whenever I am feeling down I pray the Lord strengthens my faith and draws me closer and closer to Himself so I remain stronger in my faith and pray for all my family and relatives. I continue to pray every day and trust in His grace. I believe what I am going through is to make a way for them and even others to come into the house of the Lord according to His will. Amen.

CHAPTER 21

EVICTION

The tribulation continued, and a couple of months after the death of my mother I suffered a different kind of tribulation on my return home. This time I faced eviction from my house because of the accumulated rent arrears which had built up when I took up maternity leave from work for six month., I eventually lost my job as the Centre I once worked with lost its contract with the main College, CONEL. as a result of this it had to be closed down just six months after I had taken maternity leave. For this reason I could not keep up with my normal bills, especially my rent, let alone the loan that I had taken two years earlier which needed to be paid. So my rent arrears built up to a large amount and just before I went away for my mother's burial the problem became worse, the Housing Association could not tolerate it anymore and so they wrote to me in my absence on their intention to repossess the property. I was away so I could not reply to them as required and for this they assumed I wasn't complying, and even though I handed in evidence on my return to prove that I wasn't in the country when they wrote to me, they still obtained a Court Order for my eviction.

At Court, I tried my best to convince the Judge about my situation that I lost my job and was in part time employment which did not bring in enough income to cover everything. The housing benefit I received would be taken out from the little income I used to get and so the top up I had to pay, including a little bit for the outstanding arrears, left me with very little money to live on; and although my husband was there with me at that time and working full time, his salary was not good enough to clear the arrears as expected. Anyway, the rent was not part of his bills. So the Judge made his judgement and went ahead with the Housing Officer's request and the Court Order for my eviction was granted. I was removed from the property within two hours of the hearing, but I thank God that the Judge requested the Housing Officer to allow me some time later so I could go back into the property and gather my belongings; as it was impossible for me to clear the house I have lived in for 17 years within two hours. So the Housing Officer agreed with this and gave me some time in the following week to go and gather the rest of my belongings.

Not knowing what to do in such a limited time, the Bailiffs at Court advised me to go home quickly and only pack up the necessary items I would need before the time was up for my eviction; there were now less than two hours remaining. So I rushed home by train and gathered as much as I could for myself and the children in two suit cases, then I watched them changing my door keys and lock up the house. At that moment I became homeless and was left outside waiting for the cab with my little one, heading to the Council for assistance.

In spite of being in this situation, I trusted that the Lord was in control and He would not leave me. In fact, I felt His Presence and saw His signal when I was in the cab, I knew that He was walking with me. So I got to the Council with my younger child and my two suitcases with some clothes and necessities in them. The Council was expecting me because of my previous appointments concerning the matter, I am grateful that they received me and told me to wait there while they sorted out the temporary accommodation for me and my family. I also appreciate the effort my Council had made for me, trying to intervene with the Housing Association so that they would drop the eviction process, as they had looked at my case and found that the amount of my arrears was not great enough to require eviction. The Council had come across similar kind of cases before me, which had been resolved by the same Housing Association, and the tenants were allowed to remain in their properties, therefore why not me? But as much as they stood up for me it came to no avail, the Housing Association had determined to proceed with the eviction.

As the Council had previous knowledge about my case, some even thought what was happening was not fair, they sorted out the temporary accommodation for me that evening and I wasn't left out in the streets. However, they also informed me about the procedures, that in order for the Council to put me in the waiting list for permanent housing, they had to make sure that I hadn't made myself 'purposely homeless' therefore they would be investigating my case thoroughly.

Within about a couple of hours I was given the address details for the accommodation and was told that someone will be waiting for me with the keys when I got there. I appreciated their hospitality and thanked them for their help and called a cab and went to the place; the Lord was walking with me, I saw His signal in the sky and was contented. We waited for about 15 minutes after we got there, then the gentleman came over with the keys for my temporary home. I thanked my God and opened the door and got my stuff in. I didn't sleep there that night; I went to my daughter's a few miles away, but I moved in two days later and we all liked the place, it was like the place of rest, a three bedroom house with a clean garden and an apple tree at the back. We were happy that we had a comfortable place at the end of the trauma and I give my Council credit for their support, but we were always worried whether we would be offered a permanent place of our own in the end; and for this, I had to go through a chain of questions and papers to prove that I had not made myself homeless. In the end the Council accepted that my case was genuine and kept me on the priority list for the permanent housing.

I remained in the priority list for a while and as I continued bidding there did not appear any accommodation of interest, most were miles away from my child's school and some were in blocks of flats which I did not like. Thinking of the four bedroom house from which I had been evicted, I hoped to be moved into at least to a three bedroom house with a garden, but because I hesitated bidding for any property that was displayed on the list, I was considered not to be making an effort. Three months later I was sent a warning letter explaining that I would be given a conditional offer, which meant that I would be forced to accept an offer, otherwise I would lose even the temporary accommodation I was in and would also be taken off the priority list; and also, if I did not accept the conditional offer, it would be considered I had made myself homeless.

Two months after the warning, I was sent a conditional offer for a two bedroom flat to share with the two children, the youngest being seven years old and the older one was 19. I wondered how I could accommodate my two children at these ages in one room, so the property I was offered was actually not enough for me and my family considering the huge age difference. I queried a lot about overcrowding and the fact that I did not wish to move into a flat but I was told that the property I was offered was appropriate and if I wouldn't take it I would no longer be the Council's responsibility. The only option I had was to accept the property and appeal against the decision later, while in the property, to avoid becoming 'purposely homeless.' I knew they didn't do me justice on this but I was left with no option, so I accepted the offer and sent my appeal soon after I had moved in. Because I was appealing I could not have my belongings with me while the appeal was in the process, so everything had to remain in the storage place for as long as the case would take. However, three months later I received a letter from the Council explaining that my appeal was not accepted because I did not have sufficient grounds for moving into a larger property.

Well, there was not much I could do and in fact, I needed a break, I didn't want to over pressurise myself. Overall, it took about six month before my items were returned to me; some were lost, some were left forgotten at the house and some I gave to my neighbour during eviction.

A year and a half later while in my new property the

new Housing Association found grounds for my re-housing because of overcrowding. So they inquired about this with the Council and they eventually agreed that we are actually over-crowded in the flat, so because of this the Council have once again put me on their register for bidding but as a 'Band 4', which means that our case is no longer a priority as it was before. Having heard rumours from other people that in this Band people could remain bidding for a very long time, and some have even been waiting for almost 10 years, I really couldn't see the point of bidding, fortunately the new rules came out from the government that young people under 25 could still stay with their parents if they wished to, so because of this they moved me to Band 3. Though still not good it couldn't be worse than Band 4. Well, as I still live in this flat I have to continue bidding hoping for a three bed property that could give room for my little one so that she could do her homework in a convenient place and play with her friends in her own bedroom. How do I live then? I have to share my bedroom with my little one because the older one is now 22, they can't fit together. Do I have life then? I really don't bother about this for now, I believe what I went through is for a while; it won't be forever. Inside my heart I have put my full trust in the Lord believing that He sees everything and is in control of all. He will neither abandon me nor ever fail me, I trust Him.

CHAPTER 22

CONCLUSION

Remaining strong in Christ

As I conclude this book I remain strong in Christ and give this message to everyone seeking God or those who are in doubts, fear or bondage, 'It can be done and you can change', I have seen it in myself. Indeed there is a lot of sacrifice to take in and most of the time you may think it is the end of the world, you may be in the state of losing hope, thinking that you may not get through, but remember that God cannot take you out of something for nothing or abandon you and also His word does not go back to Him void. He said in the Book of John that He will not leave us orphans, He will come to us, John 14:18. Yes,it may take a while before we see His light shining on us but we will come out of the tunnel into the light. So don't give up and stand still in your faith in Him, put Jesus Christ first and ahead of everything in your life. Remember what He said in Psalm 46:10, before He came in flesh, 'Be still and know that I am God, I will be exalted among the nations, I will be exalted in the earth'. And therefore we pray for this end.

I did not change my faith because of marriage difficulties as was anticipated by my relatives, neither did I change it because I have lived in the Western world for so long, but because I have known God. I have found out the truth and this has made me free. I know now that Jesus Christ is the Lord our God because He told me so and He proved His word in action by revelations and wonders in visions and dreams, visits and live episodes. I believe He has also filled me with

His Holy Spirit because I also speak in tongues, though I do not boast in this. Through His appointed servant He had used to reveal Himself to me, He told me to speak in tongues and I spoke. I was shocked but it happened; the only problem was I didn't know how to stop it so I kept on talking and talking but thank God it eventually stopped by itself and since then it has been something I do naturally. I noticed, it usually happens when I'm in congregation at Church, in my private prayers or when I pray for someone. In fact, it can happen at any time, any day or place. It is so interesting. I believe this is the gift of the Holy Spirit that the Lord had said He will send to everyone who would believe in Him. Acts 2:4 says, 'And they were all filled with the Holy Spirit and begun to speak with other tongues, as the Spirit gave them utterance', so I believe it is the fulfilment of the Lord's promise He made to His disciples just before He ascended to heaven. Going back to just before I was baptised in 2003, the Lord had once asked me to read the whole chapter in John 3, and when I got to John 3:5, I came across this statement, 'Unless one is born of water and the Spirit, he cannot enter the kingdom of God.' So for me this act of speaking in tongues is the reassurance that I am not only baptised by water but also by His Spirit. Amen.

Jesus, my Lord, my God, decided to reveal Himself to me out of nothing. He gathered me from the darkness, out of the pit and took me into the light which I cannot ignore. I cannot deny Him. Through His servant He spoke to me by Scriptures, revelations and personally by visits and live conversations. Does this mean I'm in despair? I believe not, it is true that God does speak to His people and can also visit them whether in visions, dreams or by demonstrations of His miracles and wonders. He can engage with someone in direct conversations whether from above, within or around them. He does this with me and I've not lost my mind as you might think. At least most of us would know that God spoke to Moses, so He does speak, He also did this directly with many other Prophets in the past including the Patriarchs like Abraham, so even though it does not happen with everybody I believe this act still continues.

God anoints His people for different purposes and so speaks to them to fulfil His will. Jesus once said in the Scriptures, 'If I do not do the work of My Father, do not believe Me, but if I do, though you do not believe Me, believe the works, that you may know and believe that the Father is in Me, and I in Him', John 10:37-38. In John 5:39, He says, 'You search the Scriptures, for in them you think you have eternal life, and those are they which testify of Me'. So which Scriptures is He actually talking about? Basically He is referring to the Old Testament, all of it, from the beginning to the time that He came and revealed Himself in flesh; and if these Scriptures testify of Him as He claims, then the Old Testament is no longer concealed but revealed in the New Testament, and actually by Himself, the Messiah!

The Messiah, Jesus Christ, is the **only Saviour**; there is no-one else. There may have been many Prophets in the past that God had sent to us so that we could understand Him and His statutes but no one other than Jesus, **the Messiah** could have taken our sins away. Neither do daily nor yearly sacrifices or good works wash away our sins and make us holy and righteous in front of God and give us a way to Heaven, as many of us believe, but only the holy blood of the Saviour, Jesus Christ. When he saw Jesus approaching, John the Baptist said, 'Behold, The Lamb of God who takes away the sin of the world!' John 1:29. The Lamb of God is the Lord Jesus Christ who was crucified on that Cross over 2000 years ago for our sins. He was the Sacrifice for everyone once and for all. He said, 'I am the way, the truth and the life; no one comes to the Father except through Me,' John 14:6. Therefore as He says, He is the only way to Heaven for everyone, there is no other way than this. By accepting Him as our Lord and Saviour, that He died on the Cross for our sins and was buried and resurrected on the third day as He said He would, we have the promise of eternal life in Heaven; 'For God so loved the world, that He **gave** His only begotten Son, that whoever believes in Him should not perish but have everlasting life', John 3:16. So Jesus Christ is the only way to heaven, as He said, He did not come into the world to condemn it but that the world through Him might be saved, John 3:17. He has gone to prepare a place for us, and He will come again and receive us to Himself, that where He is there we may be also, John 14:2-3. I pray this is a turning point for you, and if so, I suggest a sample prayer for confession of your sins but this has to come from your own heart. The Bible says believe in your heart and confess with your mouth, Romans 10:9.

Confession prayer

Believe that Jesus Christ died for you and was buried and rose from the dead. Through prayer, invite Jesus into your life as your Lord and Saviour. Say that you accept His sacrifice as perfect and complete and ask Him to forgive you and place your trust in Him alone for your Salvation. Thank Him for giving you eternal life in Heaven and the gift of the Holy Spirit.

Once you have said this prayer, you have become a believer in Christ. You will now need to go to Church regularly and learn about your new faith and practise worship; but most importantly learn the Word of God, the Bible. You may find that there are many variations of the Bible but I found the New King James Version (NKJV) subtitled (The Spirit Filled Life Bible) easy to understand and is the nearest version from the original Hebrew Bible. The NKJV is a translation of the old English which was used in the original King James Version (KJV) to the new modern English but it preserves all the information from the old version, nothing is missed. The new version is the fourth edition from the original Hebrew Bible.

The Model Prayer

Most believers in Christ say this prayer in their daily routines in addition to all other prayers they may have in mind in their everyday life. I remember one day eleven years ago when I knew I had known my God I asked Him in my night prayer to teach me how to pray. As I finished saying the prayer and went to bed, a person appeared in my dreams with a Book in his hand. He sat down with me near my praying mattress and opened the Book. As the Book was opened, he came up to a certain page and pointed his finger to a place written in red and said to me when you want to pray this is what you say. I looked in the Book and saw the words written in red starting with, **'Our Father in Heaven'**. The man suddenly disappeared and the dream ended.

The next day I opened my Bible and searched on all the red writings in it and eventually found those first words in the Book of Matthew verses 6 to 9; but I wanted to understand the full context so I started from verse 5 to 13. In these verses Jesus said when you pray go into your room and when you have shut your door, pray to your Father who is in the secret place, and your Father who sees in secret will reward you openly. He goes on to say, and when you pray do not use vain repetitions as the heathen do, for they think that they will be heard for their many words. Therefore do not be like them, for your Father knows of the things you have need of before you ask Him. In this manner therefore pray:

'Our Father in Heaven
Hallowed be Your name
Your kingdom come
Your will be done on earth as it is in Heaven
Give us this day our daily bread and forgive us our
debts as we forgive our debtors
And do not lead us into temptation but deliver
us from the evil one
For yours is the kingdom and the power
and the glory forever
Amen.'

This is called 'The Lord's Prayer'.

Worship
Worship involves songs of praise to the Lord and in some of them the concepts are taken from the Bible; I've noticed from our Church many of these would come from the Book of Psalms but others are just normal songs for worship.

141

Depending upon the Church you will go to, some involve worship songs with musical instruments while others sing in hymns with a piano. Worships involving musical instruments is not extraordinary or strange as I first thought, it is actually Biblical and started all the way back from the Psalms of David in the Old Testament, before even Christ came to the world, it is very common in the Pentecostal Church and Biblical. The choice will be yours but the whole point is to worship God. When one person, even one person is saved from the hell fire, the Angels of God rejoice in Heaven, they praise God in Heavenly worship. We also praise God in worship by songs of praise. I personally like the ones sung in slow music. This one below is one of my favourites from Cece Winans' videos accessible from You Tube. I hope you like it:

'All to Jesus I surrender all to Him I freely give
I ever love and trust Him in his presence daily live
I surrender all, I surrender all
All to Thee my blessed Saviour
I surrender all

All to Jesus I surrender
Make me Saviour wholly thine
Let me feel the Holy Spirit truly know that thou art thine
I surrender all, I surrender all
All to Thee my blessed Saviour
I surrender all

All to Jesus I surrender Lord I give myself to thee
Feed me with thy love and power let thy blessing fall on me
I surrender all I surrender all
All to Thee my blessed Saviour
I surrender all

PART TWO

In my second book I will give you updates on my progress as I grow in the Kingdom of God as a child of God and how I maintained my faith in Jesus Christ. I will write from where I finished this book and talk about the new prophecies of God I have received from the same person He had used. I will update you on how the Lord changed my entire life to the one He wanted me to be from the beginning. I will explain how I responded to His call and become obedient to Him despite my predicaments. You will find out how the Lord is working in my life and my family and the progress of my relationship with them since my rejection by them and my position towards them as a Christian. Until then rejoice in the name of the Lord. Amen.